Taking the Boat: **The Irish in Leeds, 1931-81**

Published by: **Brendan McGowan**, 19 Woodview Court, Killala, Co. Mayo, Ireland.

Email: **takingtheboat@hotmail.com**

Text copyright: © **Brendan McGowan 2009**

Font Cover Image: **iStockPhoto**

Design, layout and typesetting:
Barry Jordan at **Spear Design**, www.speardesign.ie

Printing & Reprographics: **Castleprint** Galway Ltd

An Chomhairle Oidhreachta
The Heritage Council

spear | design

LEEDS IRISH care
HEALTH & HOMES culture
community

IrishArts
Foundation
Ó aois go nua-aois:
Ag ceiliúradh na
nGlanealt Éireannach
sa Bhreatain

From the Traditional
to the Innovative:
Celebrating the Arts
of Ireland in Britain

Paperback Edition ISBN: **978-0-9563757-0-4**
Hardback Edition ISBN: **978-0-9563757-1-1**

This work would not have been possible without contributions in money and kind by Heritage Council, Irish Arts Foundation, Leeds Irish Health & Homes, Mayo County Council and Spear Design.

contents

Acknowledgements

During the course of researching, writing and publishing of this book many debts have been incurred. First and foremost, I am eternally grateful to all those who invited me into their homes and shared with me so openly their life stories; I hope that I have used your testimony in a way that is respectful and truthful.

My sincere thanks are due to John Tunney, who supervised the MA thesis on which this book is based, for his support, encouragement and guidance.

The assistance given by Ant Hanlon, Anna Dunne and all at the Leeds Irish Health and Homes was truly invaluable – thanks to all. Thanks to Austin Vaughan and Mayo County Council for deeming the book worthy of their financial support. Thanks to Patrick O'Sullivan, University of Bradford, for putting pen to paper, or digits to keyboard, for the foreword. Thanks to Gemma Marren whose keen eye and editorial skills turned thesis into book. Particular thanks to Barry Jordan of Spear Design whose artistic talent and enthusiasm have produced this book.

I am also indebted to the following people for their help without which this book would not have been possible: Fionnula Bourke, Central Bank and Financial Services, Dublin; Caitríona Clear, National University of Ireland, Galway; Richard and Betty Conway; Ciarán Counihan, Central Statistics Office, Dublin; Robert Finnegan, Leeds Diocesan Archives; James Gavaghan; Des Hurley and Chris O'Malley, Irish Arts Foundation; Danny and Helen Kennally, Leeds Irish Historical Society; Tommy McLoughlin, Leeds Irish Centre; Councillor Gerry Murray; and Corinne Silva.

Thanks to Leeds City Library for allowing me to reproduce their archive photographs, and also Ultan Cowley for allowing me to use documents from his archive. Thanks too to the library staff at the Galway-Mayo Institute of Technology and National University of Ireland, Galway.

On a personal level I would like to thank my parents, James and Irene, who instilled in me from an early age an interest in the Irish in Leeds with vivid stories of a vibrant community. My brother and sisters, Declan, Leona and Sinead, were each in their own particular way supportive. My grandmother, Ellen Ferguson, who emigrated from Mayo and spent three decades living in Leeds, was always ready to impart with stories and was an invaluable source of reference. Thanks to Vicky for love and friendship, and for being so understanding throughout.

A sincere and especial thank you to 'my second family' – John, Mary, Seán, Ellie, James and Martin Gavaghan and Ciarán 'the lodger' Ferguson – who made me feel so at home on my many trips to Leeds (your hospitality and friendship will not be forgotten). Thanks, too, to John and Maureen Ferguson and Bernard Dwyer who provided encouragement and insightful information.

Many friends provided sound advice, invaluable support and necessary distraction during the two years it took to complete this study: Darren Coyne, Raymond Coyne, Mike Diamond, Ian W. Davis, James Dineen, Eoin Donoghue, Bob Hennigan, Leroy Marshall, Gerry Martin, Lee McDaid, Colm McLoughlin, Ross Molloy and John Rafter. Particular thanks to John 'Lovely Guinness' Burke for overt criticism, wise counsel, editorial skills and friendship.

Finally, this work is dedicated to the memory of my grandfather, Martin 'Greasaí' Ferguson.

Glossary of Terms

Term	Literal Translation	Explanation
Comhaltas Ceoltóirí Éireann	Commonwealth of musicians/ singers of Ireland	An Irish traditional music organisation
Caint na ndaoine	Language of the People	The common spoken language; in this case Hiberno-English
Culchie	Shortened version of 'agricultural' or a person from Kiltimagh (Coillte Mach), Co. Mayo	A derogatory name for a person from rural Ireland
Dáil	Assembly	House of Representatives of the Irish Parliament
Éire	Ireland	Ireland
Fianna Fáil	Soldiers of destiny	Ireland's largest political party founded in 1926 by Eamonn de Valera
Fine Gael	Family of the Gael	Ireland's second largest political party founded in 1933 by the amalgamation of a number of parties
Fleadh Cheoil (na Breataine)	Festival of music (of Britain)	Traditional Irish music festival
Gardaí	Guards	Irish Police Force
Scoraíocht(aí)	Social evening(s)	Evening(s) of Irish traditional entertainment
Shant, also Shanty	Old house	A seasonal migrant workers temporary accommodation; from the Gaelic sean tigh, meaning old house.
Spalpeen, also spailpín	Seasonal agricultural labourer, also a rascal/scamp	An agricultural labourer who travelled about the country or abroad at certain seasons seeking work. Now pejorative.
Tattie hoker, also Tatie-howker	Potato digger	A (migrant) potato digger. Tattie (corruption of potato) and hoker (variant of holker, holk, a verb meaning to hollow out by digging, to dig up or dig out)
Tánaiste	Heir, successor	Deputy Prime Minister
Taoiseach	Chief, ruler	Prime Minister
Townland	Townland	The smallest administrative division of land in Ireland

Foreword
By Patrick O'Sullivan

For those who study the Irish Diaspora, these are interesting times. When, some decades ago, I first began to survey the historiography of the Irish Diaspora, I discovered a mixed research record, of varying quality. By contrast, we now have a substantial amount of good work, within many academic disciplines. Further, through formal and informal organisations, and through new resources on the internet, we are much more aware of the work that exists – which means that we are also aware of gaps in the research record, and we are aware of research resources and research opportunities.[1]

There are still gaps in the research record, of course – with some themes shaped, not by the stories that we had to tell, but by the stories that we were allowed to tell, or the stories our listeners wanted to hear. Opportunities are constrained by limited resources, of expertise, time and money. Scholars of the other diasporas, when they approach us for information or in the hope of co-operation, are always amazed to learn that there is so little in the way of an organisational structure to support and encourage the study of the Irish Diaspora. And, when it comes to listing research resources, the story is often bleak. Many possible research resources are simply disappearing.

I can give examples. One day in the early 1970s, in Melbourne, Australia, Bernard Slattery visited his aged mother, in whose home had collected generations of family documents and memorabilia. 'So Mum was left with all that stuff and she decided she'd have a bonfire in the backyard. She was sitting there ... throwing the stuff into the fire ... It was a mound. Taller than us ... Unfortunately, an awful lot of stuff was destroyed but we can't blame Mum'.[2] Among the items saved from that fire by Bernard was a sampler, a piece of needlework.

The history of that needlework sampler, its making and its significance, has been pieced together by Brian Lambkin, of the Centre for Migration Studies, Omagh, and his colleagues. The sampler was made in Ireland in 1850 by Dorcas McGee, the sister of Thomas D'Arcy McGee. Thomas D'Arcy McGee's flight from Ireland in 1848 took him first to the United States, then to Canada, where he became one of the 'Fathers of Confederation' of Canadian historiography. Evidently Dorcas McGee took the sampler with her, when she emigrated to Australia in 1852. The design of the sampler incorporates a poem, 'The Irish Chiefs' by Charles Gavan Duffy, first published in 1846. The subject matter and the design suggest that Dorcas McGee thought of her brother as one of those lost 'Irish Chiefs'.

As Brian Lambkin has shown, the meaning of the sampler was lost, as the generations passed, until the sampler itself was very nearly lost to that bonfire. We do not know what else was lost in the fire. This sampler has become an icon of the Irish Diaspora, almost literally an icon. For everything we associate with the word 'icon' is there. The sampler was made with love, knowledge and prayer. It contains history, and it can only be understood through study. And it is now preserved inside a glass case. But the sampler is only one example of many. I could tell the story of Roger André, a university archivist in Adelaide, who took his boxes to the recycling depot, idly looked at some bundles of documents already left there – and realised that he was looking at the nineteenth-century archives of the Orange Order of New South Wales.[3] Or of the young Irish scholar, Siobháin Maguire, who drove around in her little

If our archives, memorabilia and artefacts are being lost we are at the same time losing some things even more precious – the memories, experiences and emotions of our people.

car to collect the archives of the 1970s Irish organisations in Britain, as the organisations' members died or went into care homes. The plain truth is that throughout the world the possible research archives of the Irish Diaspora are disappearing into bonfires and skips.

If our archives, memorabilia and artefacts are being lost we are at the same time losing some things even more precious – the memories, experiences and emotions of our people. Scholars of other diasporas, our colleagues, are always surprised to be told that the main destination for Irish emigrants in the twentieth century was not the very visible United States of America, but Ireland's neighbouring island, Britain. Throughout the twentieth century there were never less than half a million Ireland-born people in Britain. In 1971 the number was just short of one million. Where, our colleagues ask, is this huge emigration and settlement visible in the research record? Every major city in the United States has its study of the Irish. We have nothing comparable in Britain. The reasons for this gap are complex – they are political and cultural, and practical. The material is there to be studied.

So, I am saying that there is much work to be done. And, of course, in saying that there is work be done, I am also saying that someone must do the work. Looking back at my own notes, I see that it was towards the end of 2002 that I was first contacted by Brendan McGowan, with an outline of his plan to develop an oral history study of the Irish of Leeds, and a request for help. We get quite a few requests of this sort, and we do always try to be helpful – but, frankly, we do not expect that many will lead to great things. Sometimes it is sufficient that there is simply one more person in the world with a bit of knowledge about the Irish Diaspora, and how it is studied.

Now that Brendan McGowan's study is complete, I am impressed at how well he has done, and how well he has been served by his support structures at the Galway-Mayo Institute of Technology. Of the introductions that I made for Brendan McGowan perhaps the most important was the connection established with Ant Hanlon of Leeds Irish Health and Homes, a voluntary organisation which supports the Irish community in Leeds. The Irish voluntary organisations in Britain have to tread a difficult path, and I think that it is a special strength of Ant Hanlon's vision that he sees heritage and culture as part of welfare.

One inspiration for Brendan McGowan was a recently published book by Sharon Lambert, about Irish women in Lancashire. Sharon Lambert, simply by listening to our people, has made visible, made heard, some of the tensions that we have to carry within ourselves. Maura, born in 1927, in Roscommon, told Sharon Lambert, 'They taught us to hate England and then they sent us here.'[4] Ireland since the 1990s has become a country that no longer needs to export its own people – no one in the Irish Diaspora wishes things otherwise. There is a danger that the threads which hold us together, the web of family and affinity, will fray and snap. And maybe this is inevitable – the study of other diasporas tells us this.

I have said that Brendan McGowan's study is complete. In my view research of this kind is not complete until it is published, and has been given back to the people. This he has now done, with the publication of this book. The Irish of Leeds, like the Irish of New York or Boston, now have their book. Brendan McGowan has given the Irish of Leeds their place in the research record – he has made a significant contribution to the research literature of the Irish Diaspora. And he has given the city of Leeds a better understanding of itself.

Notes

1 Patrick O'Sullivan, 'Developing Irish Diaspora Studies: A Personal View', *New Hibernia Review*, 7, no. 1, 2003, pp. 130–148.

2 Brian Lambkin and Jennifer Meegan, 'The Fabric of Memory, Identity and Diaspora: An Irish Needlework Sampler in Australia with United States and Canadian Connections', *Folk Life*, 43, 2005, pp. 7–31.

3 David Fitzpatrick, 'Exporting Brotherhood: Orangeism in South Australia', *Immigrants & Minorities*, 23, 2005, pp. 277–310.

4 Sharon Lambert, *Irish Women in Lancashire, 1922–1960*, Lancaster: Centre for North–West Regional Studies, University of Lancaster, xii, 2001, p. 129.

Introduction

Emigration is a theme in Irish history that touches almost every family in Ireland. In particular, it has been a central thread of the relationship between Ireland and Britain.[1]

All too often migration is viewed solely as a movement of population which is subject to rigorous quantitative analysis. But the process of migration involves real people with real stories... By 1971 the Irish born population was the largest migrant grouping in Britain, yet relatively little is known about the actual experience of these migrants. Further studies using oral testimony and documentary sources should begin the process of unravelling this complex and nuanced facet of the Irish migrant experience.[2]

This study of the Irish in Leeds bears testament to those who left Ireland for Britain in what is often referred to as the second great wave of Irish emigration; the first wave roughly coincides with the nineteenth century. In contrast to Irish emigrants in nineteenth-century Britain, those in the twentieth century have received little academic attention; instead the focus has tended towards Afro-Caribbean and Asian immigration at the expense of those of longer standing and greater numbers but perhaps of less visibility.[3] As Enda Delaney highlighted above, little is known about the actual Irish emigrant experience in the twentieth century. As a small step towards correcting this deficiency this study, using oral history and life narratives, examines common elements of the emigration experience: the actual emigration process, the initial settlement period, post-emigration contact with home and the issue of permanent return to Ireland. Oral history has enabled and empowered these Irish emigrants to write *their* history, as far as possible, from their own perspective and in their own words. Although written within a Leeds context, their experiences are of great relevance to Irish emigrants throughout Britain in that the themes raised during the life narrative interviews will be familiar to the vast majority of emigrants.

The book covers the period from 1931 to 1981 and is confined to those who left the 26 counties which are independent of Britain, i.e. the Irish Free State (1922), Éire (1937) or the Republic of Ireland (1949). It focuses solely on emigrants from the Republic because for social, political and economic reasons, their situation was deemed different from those who emigrated from Northern Ireland. Why start in 1931 rather than, say, 1921 to coincide with the foundation of the Irish Free State? Oral history by its very nature requires that it be written about experiences within living memory because, as it has been so realistically put 'we cannot, alas, interview tombstones'.[4] It soon emerged from the life narrative interviews that the earliest decade of emigrating was the 1930s, and in 1931 the English and Irish censuses coincided, so this seemed an appropriate start date.

Furthermore, the 1930s are an appropriate start date for any study of the Irish in twentieth-century Britain since this decade heralded the beginning of a 'second wave' of emigration to Britain. Irish migration of the last two centuries has been neatly sub-divided into three primary temporal waves, each with its own specific features.[5] The first wave roughly begins in the 1820s and was heavily fuelled by those fleeing the Great Hunger. The primary destination was the United States, but significant numbers fled to Britain. The second wave started in the 1930s with the primary destination now England; as a result of the Depression years of the 1920s and the subsequent series of restrictions imposed by the United States on immigration Ireland's nearest island neighbour gradually became the main destination for its emigrants. The 1931 census recorded 381,089 Irish-born persons residing in England and Wales; in 1951 this figure had risen to 627,021. The 1970s witnessed the end of this second wave as Ireland unexpectedly achieved a net back-flow of migrants. A third or 'new wave' of emigration took place throughout the 1980s. Therefore the period covered by this study neatly coincides with the second wave of emigration from 1931 to 1981.

Before proceeding any further, it is necessary to clarify the use of some terms which appear throughout. Until the 1921 British census everyone born on the island of Ireland was included in the Irish Born category, but from 1931 the birthplace of Irish respondents was sub-categorised into 'Northern Ireland', 'Irish Free State' (subsequently 'Irish Republic') and 'Ireland (part not stated)'. It is this last category – 'Ireland (part not stated)' – which has proved problematic in that it could not be ascertained if the respondent had been born north or south of the border. In 1961 a post-enumeration survey was carried out for the first time in order to examine information gathered during the census. On the subject of Irish birthplace the survey concluded that:

A number of persons gave the reply 'Ireland' or 'Éire' with no indication whether this referred to Northern Ireland or the Irish Republic. The people appear in certain tables in the group 'Ireland (part not stated)'. The post enumeration survey indicated that practically all these persons were actually born in the Irish Republic.[6]

In consideration of this 1961 finding, the figures shown in this book for 'Ireland (part not stated)' have been added to those of the 'Irish Republic' when giving the overall number of Irish-born in Leeds and England. Another difficulty is that it is impossible to obtain accurate figures from the British censuses for the number of Irish-born who were in Britain temporarily, such as seasonal migratory workers.

Basing nationality on place of birth is crude and problematic in that it classifies only those born on Irish soil as Irish, and not those second- and third-generation children of Irish emigrants who may consider themselves Irish.

One of the problems of using the British census, from an Irish perspective at least, is that since 1841 the censuses have defined Irishness by the birthplace of the individual. This system of basing nationality on place of birth is crude and problematic in that it classifies only those born on Irish soil as Irish, and not those second- and third-generation children of Irish emigrants who may consider themselves Irish. (The same it must be said is true for those born in Ireland of foreign-born parents.) For example, between the censuses of 1961 and 1971 Ireland experienced a population rise of approximately 32,000 children under the age of fifteen years who had been born in Britain. This unexpected increase has been explained by the fact that many Irish emigrants of the post-war years returned to Ireland with their families in the 1960s.[7] These children would by English census classification be British citizens, yet it is likely that many of them would not consider themselves so.

With regards to the actual size of the Irish community (Irish-born, their children and grandchildren) Mary J. Hickman, Professor of Irish Studies and Sociology and Director of the Institute for the Study of European Transformations at London Metropolitan University, has estimated that 'the number of Irish-born people in the Census should be multiplied by 3 to give the size of the Irish community'.[8] When this significant increase is taken into account it would, for example, increase the 1981 Irish-born population of Leeds from 7,563 to 22,689 or 3.3 per cent of the total population of Leeds.

After much campaigning by groups representing the Irish in Britain, the 2001 census for the first time included 'Irish' as an ethnic minority category. Under the question 'What is your ethnic group?' the respondent was asked to choose one section from A to E and to tick the appropriate box to indicate the choice of cultural background. Section A (White) gave the further option of ticking British, Irish or Any Other White.

There is a trend in recent studies to use the term 'migration' to describe the movement of Irish people to Britain and elsewhere. Patrick O'Sullivan, the editor of the award-winning series entitled *The Irish Worldwide*, contested that contributors to the anthology should avoid the use of 'those emotionally freighted words "emigrant" and "immigrant"'; instead he advised the use of 'the more neutral word "migrant"'.[9] However, for a variety of reasons, throughout this book 'emigrant' and 'emigration' are the words of choice used to describe those who left Ireland and their movement to Britain. During the period 1931–81 Ireland was a free and autonomous country and those who left for England were crossing international borders, regardless of freedom of movement between the two countries, therefore, the word 'emigrant' is an accurate description. Furthermore, since this is essentially an oral history based on the personal experiences, memories and opinions of Irish people in Britain, emotion is an inextricable part of these narratives. Finally, during this period 'emigrant' and 'emigration' were the common historical and contemporary terms used; these words were also favoured by the respondents themselves.

The Irish in Britain

The Irish, although the longest established and until recently the most numerous ethnic minority in Britain, have received relatively little attention within British social history or indeed the sociology of migration, race and ethnicity. However, there has been a gradual increase of interest in the Irish in Britain over the last three decades, which has been reflected in a growing body of local, regional and national studies by historians and social geographers, much of it in the form of essay compilations.[10] These works, however, primarily focus on the Irish emigrant experience during the nineteenth century when, it may be argued, the Irish were most discernible in British society. There are comparatively fewer studies on the Irish in twentieth-century Britain; this is crudely highlighted by the fact that in a bibliography of the history of the Irish in Britain published in 1986, 65 per cent of the works focus on the nineteenth-century compared with just 35 per cent on the twentieth century.[11] This disproportionate interest may be explained by the fact that the Irish in nineteenth-century Britain were regarded as a serious social problem and were subject to much contemporary official scrutiny and criticism. In a Leeds context, Dillon noted that:

Their arrival in such numbers and in such destitution is unique amongst immigrants to Britain and their presence created problems of which those resulting from twentieth-century immigrations are but a pale reflection. Animosity and misunderstanding resulted, and the Irish became, as for a long time they remained, an isolated minority.[12]

As a consequence, there is an abundance of nineteenth-century accounts of the Irish in urban Victorian Britain for the historian to draw upon, but relatively few focusing on the twentieth century. This is reflected in modern writings concerning the city of Leeds and its Irish inhabitants which rely heavily on mid nineteenth-century reports.

The Irish in Leeds are notably absent in the aforementioned compendiums in both localised studies and thematic essays. This is despite the fact that in 1861, for example, Leeds was the sixth largest town in the United Kingdom of Great Britain and Ireland (having a population of more than 207,000 of which 5 per cent were Irish born). Certainly, Leeds has not received the same attention as smaller towns with fewer Irish residents (in both absolute and relative terms).

By 1971, as a result of continual emigration in the nineteenth and twentieth centuries, the Irish constituted the largest ethnic minority in Britain.

By 1971, as a result of continual emigration in the nineteenth and twentieth centuries, the Irish constituted the largest ethnic minority in Britain. The history of the Irish in Leeds is a microcosm of this migration pattern. The city has had a significant Irish population since the 1820s, which dramatically increased throughout the 1840s but petered out as the nineteenth-century drew to a close; this roughly coincides with what is termed the 'first wave' of Irish emigration. However, the 'second wave' of Irish emigration to Leeds, which took place between the 1930s and the 1970s, is the primary focus of this book.

The depiction of the Irish community in Leeds tends to be fairly negative in recent histories of the city. The most authoritative account, Steven Burt and Kevin Grady's *The Illustrated History of Leeds*, deals with the Irish in Leeds throughout the Victorian period, but particularly between the years 1832 and 1867. The former year marks a cholera outbreak in Leeds (the first victim was a two-year-old child of Irish immigrants) and the latter marks the subduing of a potentially violent Irish protest procession.[13] In similar fashion Fraser's *History of Modern Leeds* deals with the Irish in a Victorian context again focusing on religious and political differences.[14] Dr David Thornton's *Leeds: The Story of a City* also tends to focus on the negative aspects of the Leeds Irish community.[15] None of the aforementioned authors attempted to explain or to understand the reasons for the Irish situation. Notably, there is no mention of the Irish in Leeds in the twentieth-century in any of these works.

Oral History and Life Narratives

Oral history is based on the interviewing of those who have witnessed past events whose memories and reminiscences can be used for the purposes of historical reconstruction. It offers the possibility of revealing hidden histories not documented by traditional historical sources. All four of this author's grandparents migrated from the west of Ireland to Britain between the 1930s and the 1960s and eventually settled in the city of Leeds. Growing up, vivid tales of the Irish in Leeds were passed down through two generations of emigrant relatives but there is little in the way of documentary sources that record the experiences of this once thriving Leeds Irish population. These emigrants are counted in the censuses of Leeds but this skeletal data cannot speak of what it was like for the individuals to arrive from the rural west of Ireland to war-time or post-war Leeds, why they departed their Irish homes, why they chose Leeds as their destination, what networks they accessed to secure lodgings and employment, what opportunities and limitations they encountered across the water, what contact they kept with home, why some did and others did not return to live in Ireland. These answers can only be provided by the emigrants themselves; in consequence, oral history is the best source for such information. The experience of the individual therefore contributes to the collective history of the Irish in Leeds between 1931 and 1981 and unlike the many histories of the nineteenth-century Irish in Britain, which were written using establishment sources which viewed the Irish as a social problem, oral history enables a history to be written from the emigrant's own perspective.

One of the weaknesses of oral history is that it is of less use when trying to uncover specific information about events in history of national importance such as, for example, government elections or Immigration Acts to which the average person is remote:

Poverty in the Thirties to a woman with six children would not be in terms of coalition governments and social legislation and trade union demands, but soup kitchens, shoes for the family, the memory of a day's outing to the seaside – the common body of daily life. [16]

Thus, for the study of an immigrant population, oral history is the most appropriate source of information on the migration and settlement process, work and social networks, identity and other cultural issues through the study of daily life. The benefits of using oral testimony are manifold:

It offers the possibility of gaining information on aspects of life and work which would not otherwise be available. Second, it offers the opportunity of exploring people's ideas and beliefs about if not of the past ... Finally, it provides a valuable way of gaining insights into, and ideas about specific phenomena in the past.[17]

For these reasons life story interviews rather than other types of oral history such as single-issue testimony, which would focus on one particular aspect or period of a person's life, form the basis of this book; as life story testimony 'allows a person to narrate the story of his or her own life in all its dimensions: personal, spiritual, social and economic'.[18]

The Respondents

This book is based on the life narratives of emigrants from the Republic of Ireland and not those from the whole island of Ireland. It would be fair to say that the experiences of emigrants from either side of the border and from each side of the Northern divide would be diverse and each deserving of the particular attention that this study could not provide.

In total, thirty-three detailed life testimonies were recorded,[19] and a number of formal and informal, arranged and per chance meetings took place (about a dozen in total) with members of the Irish community in Leeds. Since oral history is a qualitative source of information the primary concern of the oral historian is not the number of interviewees but the diversity of their experiences and the quality of what they have to say. Attracting a statistically representative sample of respondents is not a concern since this would be a gargantuan if not impossible task, for several reasons. Firstly, many of Leeds' Irish population of the last seventy years have passed away. Secondly, because of the transient nature of the Irish emigrant, many of those who had resided in Leeds between 1931 and 1981 have since settled in other parts of Britain and others have returned to live in Ireland. There is also the insurmountable problem that not everyone is interested in imparting their life story to a complete or even a relative stranger and it was not desirable to force personal questions on reluctant interviewees.

In order to locate and contact suitable and willing respondents an open letter was sent to the editors of Irish local and national newspapers as well as to The *Irish Post* and *Ireland's Own*, which in particular has a more aged readership. The Leeds Irish Centre, which is a popular focal point for many Irish in Leeds,

The primary concern of the oral historian is not the number of interviewees but the diversity of their experiences and the quality of what they have to say

sells these newspapers; many others living across the water, who may not attend the centre regularly or at all, have their local paper sent weekly from Ireland. In addition, the same letter was sent to the *Yorkshire Post* and *Evening Post* but was refused because of the vast amount of similar requests from the public. However, the *Leeds Weekly*, which reaches a huge readership, did publish the appeal for respondents. The letter appealed to those born in Ireland who had emigrated, either directly or indirectly to Leeds, between 1931 and 1981 and who would be interested in talking about their life experiences for the purpose of research into Irish emigration. As this method of contact might only attract a response from a self-selected group of the Irish population, most likely people with particularly strong opinions or ideas about emigration personal contacts were also used (and at times abused) to recruit other informants who may not have otherwise volunteered. A nursing home in Leeds, which is run by an Irish couple and caters specifically for elderly Irish people, was contacted and consequently five more respondents were recruited. But perhaps the most valuable link that was made, which facilitated contact with many respondents who for various reasons, such as the inability to read or write, would not have easily been contactable, was with the Leeds Irish Health and Homes (LIHH).[20] The director and staff of the LIHH were met with on a number of occasions and it was decided that the organisation would, through their support workers, make the initial approach to potential respondents. The LIHH also placed an appeal in their monthly magazine. The response was, thankfully, fruitful. As a result of public notices, personal contacts, chance encounters and third party approaches a reasonably balanced group of respondents was achieved.

This group of thirty-three respondents who provided their life testimonies consisted of eighteen males and fifteen females, of whom nineteen hailed from the Province of Connacht, five from other western seaboard counties, five from Dublin and four from elsewhere in Ireland

This group of thirty-three respondents who provided their life testimonies consisted of eighteen males and fifteen females, of whom nineteen hailed from the Province of Connacht, five from other western seaboard counties, five from Dublin and four from elsewhere in Ireland. They initially emigrated from Ireland between 1933 and 1978 (seven emigrated in the 1930s, five in the 1940s, seven in the 1950s, eleven in the 1960s and three in the 1970s); most still reside in Leeds whilst a small number have since returned to live in Ireland. As is ideally the case, the group was made up of people from a diversity of social classes and occupations. All but one respondent was Catholic; this was less than ideal, however, given the focus on the Republic of Ireland perhaps this result was to be expected given the predominance of Catholicism in the country's society.

There are a number of important autobiographies, which were written about emigrant life in Britain in the twentieth century. Four emigrants whose experiences coincide with the period covered by this book are those of John O'Donoghue, Donall Mac Amhlaigh, John B. Keane and Sean Ó'Ciaráin.[21] There are, however, comparatively fewer emigrant accounts left by Irish females despite their constituting the greater portion of Irish emigrants in the twentieth century. The comment has also been made that female emigrants feature so rarely in the writings of their male counterparts because of 'the strong traditional division between male and female labour on small farms and the way that division continued in Britain where Irish men worked predominantly in male labour groups while Irish women went into hospitals and offices where employment was predominantly female'.[22] This makes the recording of life testimonies of female emigrants to Britain all the more important. Of the thirty-three emigrant life stories recorded for this book almost half were female.

There are, however, a number of published interviews and oral histories with Irish women in England. Rita Wall's *Leading Lives* is based on a series of interviews with nine Irish women who are for a variety of reasons famed. Mary Lennon's *Across the Water: Irish Women's Lives in Britain* is perhaps a more balanced account of the emigrant experiences of Irish women in that the stories captured are more representative. Another recently published collection of emigrant accounts worthy of note is entitled *An Unconsidered People: The Irish in London* and is an example of the diverse experiences of eleven male and female expatriates who spent part of their lives in the English capital. The themes covered by the author, such as memories of Ireland, reasons for emigrating, the emigration process, settling in an English city, the Irish social scene, work, housing, etc. are similar to those dealt with throughout the course of this book.

Conclusion

There has been little published material on the Irish in Leeds and, because of the hundred-year rule, detailed census material for the period in question will not be made available in its totality to the public for many decades. In consequence, oral evidence and personal testimony are the best possible sources to elicit social and cultural information about Irish emigrants in Leeds for the period from 1931 to 1981. The oral testimonies collected here provide detailed insights into many aspects of the Irish experience in Leeds such as settlement, social and network patterns, contact with home and return migration. Furthermore, as regards the importance of such a study, it has been noted and quoted that 'the sense of the past, at any given time, is quite as much a matter of history as what happened in it'.[23]

Notes

1 Remarks made by Mr Brian Cowen TD, former Minister for Foreign Affairs, at a reception to announce the 2004 Díon grants.

2 Enda Delaney, *Demography, State and Society: Irish Migration to Britain, 1921–71*, 2000, pp. 160 and 297.

3 For a discussion on the 'invisibility' of the Irish in post-war Britain see: Bronwen Walter, 'Irishness, Gender and Place', *Environment and Planning, Part D: Society and Space*, vol. 13, 1995, p. 36.

4 Paul Thompson, 'History and the Community', in Willa K. Baum and David K. Dunaway (eds), *Oral History: An Interdisciplinary Anthology*, 1984, note 78, p. 40.

5 See Alan Strachan, 'Post-war Irish Migration and Settlement in England and Wales, 1951–1981', in R. King (ed.), *Geographical Society of Ireland Special Publications*, 6, 1991, pp. 21–2; and Russell King, Ian Shuttleworth and Alan Strachan, 'The Irish in Coventry: The Social Geography of a Relict Community', *Irish Geography*, vol. 22, no. 2, 1989, p. 65.

6 Census 1961, England and Wales, Birthplace and Nationality Tables, p. xi.

7 Donal Garvey, 'The History of Migration Flows in the Republic of Ireland', *Population Trends*, no. 39, 1985, p. 25.

8 Hickman and Walter Report, *Discrimination and the Irish Community in Britain*, 1997, p. 20.

9 Patrick O'Sullivan (ed.), *The Irish Worldwide. Volume 4: Irish Women and Irish Migration*, 1995, p. 2.

10 Roger Swift and Sheridan Gilley (eds), *The Irish in Britain, 1815–1939*, 1989; Roger Swift and Sheridan Gilley (eds), *The Irish in Victorian Britain: The Local Dimension*, 1999; Patrick O'Sullivan (ed.), *The Irish Worldwide. Volume 1: Patterns of Migration*, 1992; Patrick O'Sullivan (ed.), *The Irish Worldwide. Volume 2: The Irish in the New Communities*, 1992; Patrick O'Sullivan (ed.), *The Irish Worldwide. Volume 3: The Creative Migrant*, 1994; Patrick O'Sullivan (ed.), *The Irish Worldwide. Volume 4: Irish Women and Irish Migration*; Patrick O'Sullivan (ed.), *The Irish Worldwide. Volume 5: Religion and Identity*, 1996; Patrick O'Sullivan (ed.), *The Irish Worldwide. Volume 6: The Meaning of the Famine*, 1997; Graham Davis, *The Irish in Britain, 1815–1914*, 1991; and Donald MacRaild, *The Great Famine and Beyond: Irish Migrants in Britain in the Nineteenth and Twentieth Centuries*, 2002.

11 Maureen Hartigan and Mary J. Hickman (eds), *The History of the Irish in Britain: A Bibliography*, 1986.

12 T. Dillon, 'The Irish in Leeds, 1851–61', *The Thoresby Miscellany*, vol. 16, 1979, p. 1.

13 Steven Burt and Kevin Grady, *The Illustrated History of Leeds*, 2002. See 'The Immigrants: The Irish and the Jews' (pp. 155–7) and 'Troubles with the Irish' (pp. 170–1). The Irish are elsewhere mentioned under sections entitled 'Crime, Prostitution and Dripping' (p. 169), 'The Poor Law' (p. 173), 'Combating Disease' (p. 174) and 'The Rise of Anglo-Catholicism and the Roman Catholics' (pp. 183–4); essentially in areas where the Irish were viewed as a serious social problem outside the control of British political or religious leaders.

14 Derek Fraser (ed.), *A History of Leeds*, Manchester University Press, 1980. In this publication the Irish and Jews are dealt with together as the primary immigrant groups in nineteenth-century Leeds (pp. 61–2); see 'Roman Catholicism in Leeds' (p. 256), 'Fenian Activity' (p. 342) and 'Political Differences' (pp. 342–3 and 348–9).1

15 David Thornton, *Leeds: The Story of a City*, 2002.

16 Melvyn Bragg, *Speak for England*, 1976, p. 7, quoted in Paul Thompson's *The Voice of the Past: Oral History*, 1978, p. 158.

17 D. Gittens, 'Oral History, Reliability and Recollection', in L. Moss and H. Goldstein (eds) *The Recall Method in Social Surveys*, pp. 82–97.1

18 Hugo Slim, Paul Thompson, et al., 'Ways of Listening', in Robert Perks and Alistair Thompson (eds), *The Oral History Reader*, 1998, p. 116.

19 It would appear that there is no specific number of informants that would constitute a normal or average sample for an oral history study. Both Caitríona Clear and Sharon Lambert, using oral history as their prime sources, interviewed 40 people during the course if their research; see Caitríona Clear, *Women of the House: Women's Household Work in Ireland 1922–1961*, 2000 and Sharon Lambert, *Irish Women in Lancashire, 1922–1960: Their Story*, 2001. In other works, The Irish in London was based on the sole voice and life story of Paddy Fahy, as recorded by Bernadette Halpin. Another more recent publication entitled *An Unconsidered People: The Irish in London* was founded on the emigrant experiences of eleven Irish men and women.

20 Established in 1996, Leeds Irish Health and Homes offers culturally sensitive housing and support services.

21 John O'Donoghue, *In a Strange Land*, 1958; Donall Mac Amhlaigh, *An Irish Navvy: The Diary of an Exile*, 2003; John B. Keane, *Self-portrait*, 1964; and Sean Ó'Ciaráin, *Farewell to Mayo: An Emigrant's Memoirs of Ireland and Scotland*, 1991.

22 Bernard Canavan, 'Story-tellers and Writers: Irish Identity in Emigrant Labourers' Autobiographies, 1870–1970', in O'Sullivan (ed.), *The Irish Worldwide. Volume 3: The Creative Migrant*, note 40, p. 169.

23 Raphael Samuel, *Theatres of Memory*, Vol. 1: Past and Present in Contemporary Culture, 1994, p. 15, quoted in Clear, *Women of the House*, p. 218.

Quarry Hill flats and St Patrick's Church, Burmantofts, 1968.
Courtesy of Leeds Library & Information Services

1. The Social, Historical and Geographical Context

Introduction

Leeds is nestled in the Aire Valley of West Yorkshire, east of the Pennines, in north-central England. The modern city spans the River Aire, which meanders south-eastwards across the English midlands eventually finding its way into the North Sea. Leeds lies between one of England's most important manufacturing regions to the west and agricultural regions to the north and east and is the regional capital of the Yorkshire and Humber region. Leeds is also located approximately mid-way between the capital cities of London and Edinburgh and between the Irish and North Seas, Merseyside and Humberside. Its population – 715,402 in 2001 – makes it the second largest Metropolitan District in the United Kingdom.

Leeds officially became a city in 1893. Up until 1911 the borough of Leeds and the parish of Leeds were coterminous; they consisted of the in-township of Leeds and the eleven out-townships of Armley, Beeston, Bramley, Chapel Allerton, Farnley, Headingley, Holbeck, Hunslet, Osmondthorpe, Potternewton and Wortley. In 1911 Leeds borough had a population of 445,550; the out-townships containing nearly two-thirds of this population were gradually merged with the in-township of Leeds. During the period 1912 to 1957 the city's administrative boundaries were stretched to increase the area of the County Borough by 80 per cent; Roundhay, Shadwell, Crossgates, Seacroft, Temple Newsam and Austhorpe were added to the east, Adel and Alwoodley to the north and Middleton to the south. The new City of Leeds Metropolitan District was created in 1974 as a result of local government reorganisation in England. Boundaries were extended further in all directions forming an administrative area of 216 sq. miles and 743,300 inhabitants. It was to be the second largest Metropolitan District in England (after Doncaster) and the second largest in population (after Birmingham).[1]

Far back in history Roman, Viking and Norman influxes left their mark on Leeds. More recently, in roughly successive order, the Irish, Russian and Polish Jews, Indian, Pakistani, Bangladeshi, African, Caribbean and Chinese peoples have accrued and settled in this ever-sprawling pluralist city. The story of the Irish in Leeds is broadly a historical one and is inextricably entwined with the roller-coaster fortunes of the industrial economy of the city. This chapter, by focusing on two centuries of Irish influx and influence in the city of Leeds, will create a contextual background for the entire study.

Leeds in geographical context

NORWAY

GLASGOW

EDINBURGH

IRELAND

LEEDS

LIVERPOOL

MANCHESTER

NETHERLANDS

GERMANY

BELGIUM

BRISTOL

LONDON

LUXEMBOURG

FRANCE

The Metropolitan
District of Leeds

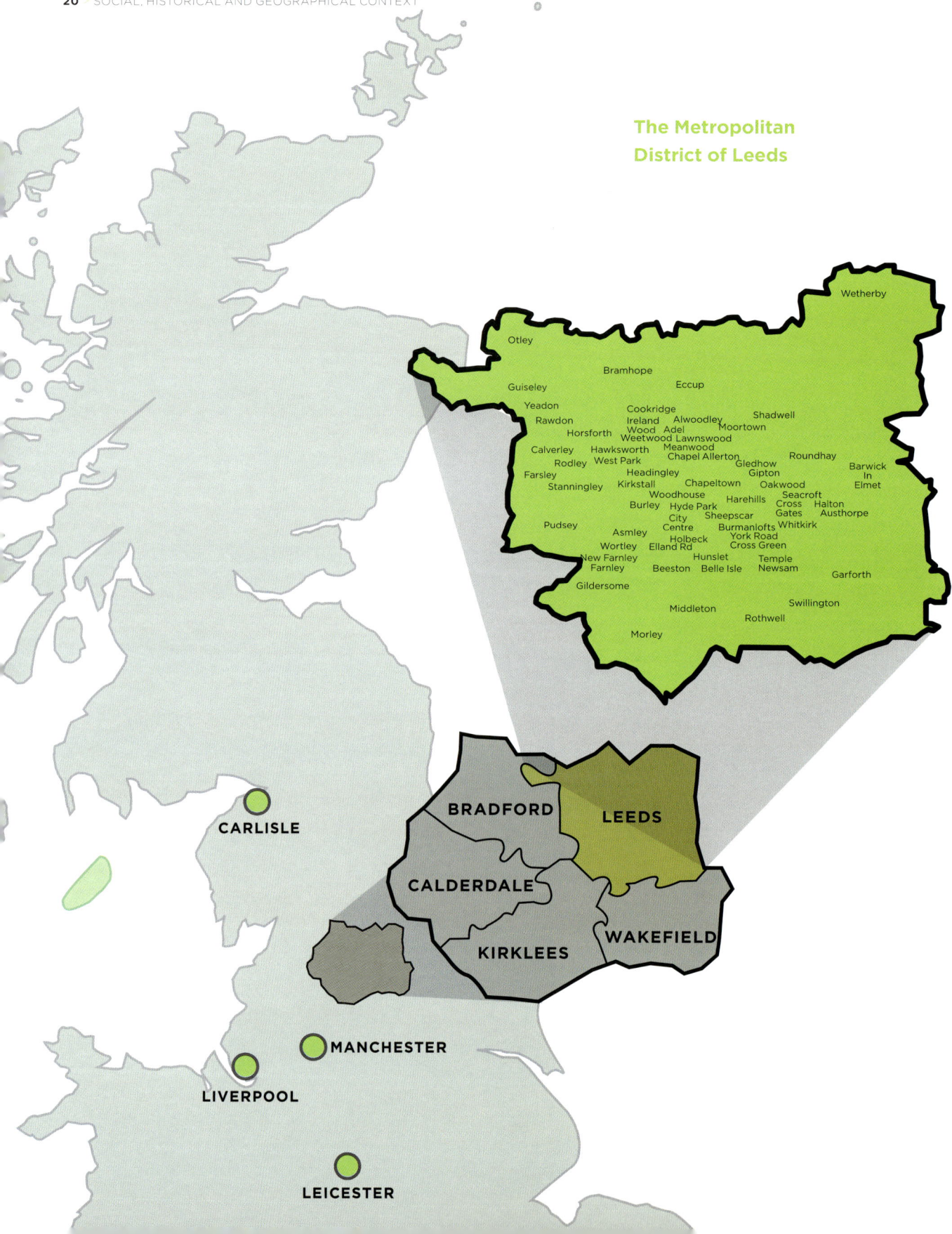

Wetherby

Otley

Bramhope

Guiseley   Eccup

Yeadon
            Cookridge
Rawdon   Ireland Alwoodley Shadwell
Horsforth   Wood Adel Moortown
         Weetwood Lawnswood
Calverley Hawksworth Meanwood
Rodley West Park   Chapel Allerton   Roundhay
Farsley   Headingley   Gledhow Gipton   Barwick
     Stanningley Kirkstall   Chapeltown Oakwood   In
                Woodhouse   Seacroft   Elmet
              Burley Hyde Park Harehills Cross Halton
                 City Sheepscar Gates Austhorpe
Pudsey   Centre Burmanlofts Whitkirk
         Asmley   Holbeck York Road
         Wortley Elland Rd Cross Green
       New Farnley   Hunslet   Temple
         Farnley Beeston Belle Isle Newsam   Garforth
Gildersome

                Swillington
        Middleton
              Rothwell
      Morley

BRADFORD   LEEDS

CALDERDALE

              WAKEFIELD

        KIRKLEES

CARLISLE

MANCHESTER

LIVERPOOL

LEICESTER

A Brief History of the Irish in Leeds Pre-1931

From the early seventeenth century the woollen trade became Leeds' main industry. The eighteenth century bore witness to the strengthening of Leeds both industrially and economically as a result of this thriving textile industry. The many coalmines in the vicinity of Leeds fuelled its numerous textile factories, which attracted labour from the surrounding countryside thus transforming this rural township into an immense industrial city. In Yorkshire in the early eighteenth century large villages with a domestic woollen trade grew at such a pace that by the mid-nineteenth century they had become sizeable towns and cities, the centre of a number of wards, which were previously villages on the periphery of the old town. Leeds is a prime example of this expansion, the population of Leeds stood at 30,309 in 1775, 53,162 in 1800, increasing rapidly to 152,054 in 1841.[2] This increase in population was primarily as a result of rural migration from the Yorkshire Dales; however, the 1841 census recorded just over 5,000 Irish-born persons living in Leeds, constituting 3.3 per cent of the total population. No doubt many of these Irish emigrants had arrived as navvies on the construction of the Leeds–Liverpool Canal (1770–1816) and the railways (1834–49), which linked the heartland of industrial Yorkshire with the Irish Sea.[3] Others perhaps began as seasonal migrants to the farms around Yorkshire and gradually gravitated towards Leeds attracted by its employment opportunities – in the woollen and textile industries, in engineering and coal mining. Again others would have been enticed to follow family, friends and neighbours who had gone before them in a process known as chain migration.

In the early 1800s open cast coal was produced at Temple Newsam, about five kilometres from Leeds. Many Irish were employed at the pit and on the railway, which took workers from Cross Green to Temple Newsam and coal to Cross Green on the return journey for distribution. The line became known locally as the 'Paddy Line'.[4] Many Irish who arrived during the 1820s and 1830s were handloom weavers who, following the domestic decline of rural textiles from the late eighteenth century, had begun to descend upon Yorkshire and Lancashire; by the 1830s two-thirds of the 900 weavers in the township of Leeds were Irish.[5] By 1838 there were said to be more than a hundred woollen mills in Leeds employing nearly 10,000 people. A number of these weavers were from Co. Tipperary, many of the other emigrants were from the western seaboard counties and their wives and children took up work in the nearby mills. By 1855 there were thirty-seven flax mills in Leeds employing a total of 9,500 workers, many of whom were Irish famine refugees, and a decade later it was noted by Alderman Carter that Irish female labour dominated the lowest strata of the labour force: 'English girls have almost entirely got into better occupations, and those flax mills, where there is such a large amount of dust and heat and steam, are filled almost entirely with the children of the lowest class of people – they are nearly all Irish now'.[6]

The working classes resided in clearly defined areas in nineteenth-century Leeds. In 1839, the Statistical Committee of the Town Council estimated that of the total population of 82,120 in the township 61,212 were of the working class.[7] The North, North East and Kirkgate wards, along with the rapidly expanding out-

The 1841 census recorded just over 5,000 Irish-born persons living in Leeds, constituting 3.3 per cent of the total population.

townships of Holbeck and Hunslet, formed the most densely populated working-class area; the middle classes tended to occupy the healthier and better situated areas in the Mill Hill, West and North West wards.[8] Thus, the division between the classes was reinforced by geographical isolation. It is estimated that in 1851 and 1861 more than 80 per cent of the Irish resided in three wards, that of the East, the North and the North East.[9] These emigrants predominantly settled in two districts (the Bank and Kirkgate) on the east bank of the River Aire forming an 'Irish Quarter' or 'Little Ireland'. These areas consisted of an area roughly enclosed by York Road to the north, the River Aire to the south, Ellerby Lane and Devon Street to the east and Vicar Lane to the west. An analysis of the census returns for 1861 highlights this Irish contingent in the east end of Leeds. Baxter's Yard, for example, had a high density of Irish emigrants and was one of the most notorious streets in Victorian Leeds; in 1861, numbers 1–13 Baxter's Yard contained Irish inhabitants. Another street with a high Irish concentration, which was frequently castigated by critics, was Dufton's Yard; in 1861, numbers 1–3, 5–11, 14–18 and 20–25 Dufton's Yard contained Irish inhabitants. The houses in this area of Leeds were back-to-backs, separated from their opposing buildings by narrow ash-covered streets, which were rarely cleaned by day or lit by night. These houses had neither gardens nor yards and opened directly onto the street so that:

The intersection of the street with clothes-lines is an anomaly in street regulations. In the township of Leeds, out of the total number of 586 streets, 276, or nearly one-half are weekly so full of lines and linen as to be impassable for horses and carriages, and almost for foot-passengers.[10]

The area was also characterised by the poor drainage and sanitation; a report by the Town Council in 1839 highlighted the fact that for a hundred dwellings inhabited by more than 450 persons there were but two privies.[11] These houses consisted of two storeys with a cellar, the window of which was visible at pavement level. Frederick Engels visited the Bank, which he recalled, in *The Conditions of the Working Class in England*, had 'drainless streets, mud a foot thick [and] cellars which were seldom dry'.[12] In addition factory pollution was problematic; the numerous red-brick chimneys of the mills and factories omitted thick plumes of smoke, which caused an almost permanent fog to engulf the city. This fog blackened the city's buildings and caused untold harm to the inhabitants living in the vicinity of these manufactories, which included most of the township's Irish population.

The old St Patrick's Church, situated on a plot of land part enclosed by York Road, Rider Street and Burmantofts Street, was built in 1831 to serve the Irish population of East Leeds. However, the rapid influx of famine refugees from Ireland in the late 1840s greatly swelled the Catholic population of the area, in particular that of the Bank district and around Richmond Hill. To meet the religious requirements of the Irish community a second larger church was built in the heart of the Bank. The building of Mount St Mary's Catholic Church was a task of gargantuan proportions, especially for an

These emigrants predominantly settled in two districts (the Bank and Kirkgate) on the east bank of the River Aire forming an 'Irish Quarter' or 'Little Ireland'.

impoverished and much despised community, and the construction was not without its tragedies and setbacks. Mount St Mary's was completed in 1857 and served the city's Irish population for more than a century.

The Great Hunger

The mass famine exodus from Ireland doubled Leeds borough's Irish-born population from 5,027 in 1841 to 10,333 in 1861. Of course the Leeds Irish community was much larger. Dillon, in his article 'The Irish in Leeds: 1851–61', has taken the term Irish to mean 'Irish-born, the children of parents one of whom at least was Irish-born, and second generation Irish, who by their names and presence within an Irish household can be recognised as the off-spring of some earlier immigrant' thus arriving at a figure of 14,905 'Irish' in the in-township of Leeds in 1861.[13] In terms of size the in-township of Leeds extended 'some three miles long from East to West and one and a half miles long from North to South'.[14] Hugh Heinrick reporting for *The Nation* in 1872 estimated a Leeds Irish population of between 22,000 and 25,000, contesting that the Irish-born population of Britain should be doubled to obtain this truer figure for its ethnic Irish population.[15]

The bulk of this post-famine colony also resided in the Kirkgate and Bank districts of Leeds. The Bank, in particular, became synonymous with poverty, disease, crime, rioting, underemployment and unemployment in contemporary writings thus reflecting the typical 'British upper and middle-class alarm concerning the mass-urbanisation of Victorian Britain and the heavy concentration of destitute Irish people in northern towns, particularly during and after the famine'.[16] There are many grim contemporary reports and first-hand accounts that highlight the harsh realities that faced Irish emigrants in their new urban homes. Even before the Irish famine refugees had arrived in great numbers, the miserable conditions of the Irish poor in Leeds were being noted; in 1842 Robert Baker a Leeds surgeon and factory inspector reported that:

In the houses of the Irish poor... there is a general state of desolation and misery. Whether it is the improvidence of the Irish character, or that their natural habits are filthy, or both, or whether there exists the real destitution which is apparent in their dwellings, I know not; but in them there is more penury, and starvation, and dirt, than in any class of people I have ever seen.[17]

Working-class conditions in Leeds in the 1840s can, without exaggeration, be described as sub-human, a statement which is supported by Edwin Chadwick, the Secretary to the Poor Law Commissioners and an ardent sanitary reformer, who reported that for every 1,000 children born in the town, 570 died before the age of five.[18]

Almost without exception, in towns of rapid economic growth in north-central England – Bradford, Leeds, Liverpool and Manchester – the Irish were rooted

The mass famine exodus from Ireland doubled Leeds borough's Irish-born population from 5,027 in 1841 to 10,333 in 1861.

firmly to the lowest rung of the economic ladder and at the mercy of low wages and underemployment.[19] Thus they relied for subsistence on their fellow working-class neighbours, on charity, on the Poor Law and occasionally on petty crime. For the March quarter of 1846, it is recorded that the number of Irish-born persons relieved by Leeds Union was 756. In the corresponding quarter for 1847, this figure increased dramatically to 3,120. There were also quite dramatic increases in other West Yorkshire Unions for the same period: Bradford from 567 to 1,428 Irish-born persons; Dewsbury 58 to 592; Halifax 194 to 2,066; Huddersfield 136 to 544; Keighley 1 to 247; Sheffield 178 to 859; and Skipton 0 to 899.[20] In the first half of 1847 many newly arrived Irish died in the towns and cities of Britain as a result of malnutrition and associated illnesses, although exact figures are lacking. The appearance of hoards of destitute Irish on the streets of urban Britain and the many newspaper reports of the desperate situation in Ireland greatly impacted on the middle classes and in turn resulted in the raising of private charity for the relief of the poor in Ireland. In a seven-month period in 1847 the substantial sum of £354 17s. 6d. along with forty-eight bales of clothing were received by the Society of Friends from Leeds for distribution to the poor in Ireland.[21] For the same period only London provided a more generous donation. The British Relief Association was even more accomplished in amassing subscriptions for the suffering in Ireland. In 1847, the British Relief Association established relief committees throughout England, which held fundraising meetings; Leeds' donations amounted to £2,500.[22]

Reverend Edward Jackson's recollections of 1847 Leeds provide a vivid and horrific first-hand account of the famine-fleeing Irish:

Tall men, with long coats and hats without crowns, and women, wild and haggard, with numbers of unearthly looking children – strange beings that ran alongside of the men and women, and looked at you out of the corner of their eyes, with a sort of half frightened, half-savage expression. The usual low lodging-houses for this class of people were soon more than full, and they extemporized for themselves dwellings such as none but they would have occupied. Why the Poor Law Authorities did not bestir themselves in time, and open proper places for the reception of these wretched exiles, seems now a strange blunder. Being Irish, I suppose they were not legally chargeable to the township. But it was a great mistake and a woeful economy; for the emigrants brought with them not only hunger but death. In a short time the frightful Irish fever [typhus] was epidemic in all the lower parts of the town.[23]

Irish Fever

The Irish community in Leeds had been associated with the spread of disease long before this outbreak of typhus. A cholera epidemic, which swept across England in the early 1830s, appeared in Leeds in 1832; the first report of infection was of a two-year-old child of Irish emigrants living in the Bank. In the following six-month period the disease claimed 600 lives in 2,000 cases primarily in the East End of Leeds where the majority of Irish were concentrated.[24] Typhus, or 'Irish Fever' as it was more commonly and officially known, appeared in Leeds in 1847. As in Liverpool, the epidemic broke out initially in the town's Irish quarters and quickly spread to other quarters. Typhus spread quickly and easily in overcrowded, impoverished conditions such as was the norm in the Bank; the often deadly organism was transmitted from the affected by body lice. The Reverend Jackson in his letters and memoirs recalled the situation in the Bank district:

Here, in this district, which was one of especially Irish character, it was simply horrible. Every place above ground, and underground, was crammed with miserable, famished wretches, scarcely looking like human beings. In one cellar we counted thirty-one men, women and children, all lying on the damp, filthy floor, with only a few handfuls of straw under them; while the frightened neighbours, who would not venture inside the pestilential depth, were lowering water in buckets to allay the intolerable thirst of the miserable people.[25]

St Patrick's Church, Rider Street, Burmantofts, 1922. Courtesy of Leeds Library & Information Services

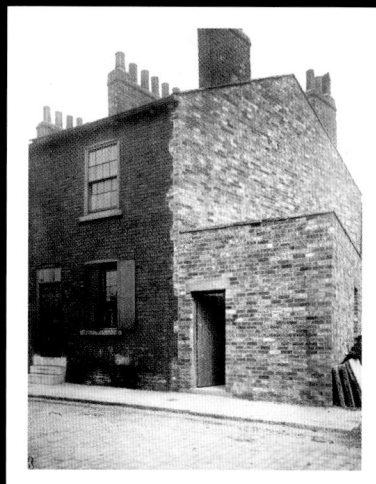

Following the gradual cessation of the typhus epidemic, cholera again returned with a vengeance in 1848 to claim 2,000 more lives in Leeds. Once more the East End of Leeds bore the brunt of the casualties. These major epidemics provoked hostility from the host community as the Irish were seen as the disseminators of these killer diseases.

In 1849, the *Morning Chronicle* journalist Angus Reach toured England reporting on the state of its major cities. He further describes the living and working conditions of some of Leeds' Irish inhabitants:

I proceeded to the neighbouring row of cottages recently erected. These had each a common room, a bedroom, and a cellar loom shop. In the first when I entered, two Irishmen were weaving a coarse sacking, and the wife of one of them was winding in the bare, scarcely furnished room on the ground floor. The tenant of the room told me that the row was all alike, and belonged to the gentleman for whom he was working. The two looms were fixtures; of course, therefore, he could not rent them without renting the house. The rent was stopped every week out of his wages. Whatever they were, much or little, the rent must always come out of them before he got his money. He believed that the work was given to him just to enable him to pay the rent (which was 3s. weekly), and thus to make a good return for the money invested in the house; otherwise it would be cheaper for the master to get the stuff woven by power. His wages, with his wife to wind, were very small, not averaging above 9s. or 10s. the highest.[26]

There is an abundance of these dire contemporary accounts.[27] And although there were as many working-class English living in the midst of this poverty, it is the Irish who were blamed for dragging the level of the neighbourhoods down. They, according to the city's officials and the media, were responsible for introducing and spreading disease, overcrowding, poor housing and poorer sanitary and drainage conditions. Edward Baines, the editor of the *Leeds Mercury*, however, pointed out that these sanitation and housing problems were not merely confined to urban areas; they were equally problematic in rural Yorkshire.[28]

According to their English fellow working-class neighbours the Irish were also responsible for lowering wage levels, whereas in fact it was unscrupulous factory employers who were taking advantage of the desperate conditions of the Irish emigrant. In retrospect, it is evident that the Irish were being used as a scapegoat for the poor conditions brought about by the Industrial Revolution and the increased population influx into Leeds from the countryside, conditions that were, for the most part, out of the control of the Irish emigrant. With this in mind it is not surprising that the Irish were not a popular grouping in mid-nineteenth-century Leeds, but with little or nothing to return home to they persevered.

The East End of Leeds, in which the Irish resided in greatest numbers, was notorious not only for its poor living conditions but also for crime, prostitution,

The East End of Leeds, in which the Irish resided in greatest numbers, was notorious not only for its poor living conditions but also for crime, prostitution, violence and drunkenness, and as a place where the police only entered in the security of numbers.

violence and drunkenness, and as a place where the police only entered in the security of numbers. Between 1851 and 1861 at least 14 per cent of all cases which came before the Leeds Quarter Sessions involved Irish persons; in 1852 the Irish accounted for 33 per cent of all assaults and breaches of the peace.[29] This situation, however, is not peculiar to Leeds; the Irish in many British urban centres such as London, Liverpool and York are over represented in certain categories of criminal offences particularly 'the often interrelated categories drunkenness, disorderly behaviour and assault (including assaults on the police) and, to a lesser extent, petty theft and vagrancy'.[30] In the more serious crimes committed, the Irish figured largely in line with the native population. Studies on criminality amongst the Irish in Britain, by Dillon for Leeds, Richardson for Bradford and Finnegan for York, have highlighted a direct relationship between crime and environmental decay.[31] In 'The Irish in Leeds, 1851–61', Dillon remarks of the Irish living in the East End of Leeds that:

In such conditions there is little wonder that the feelings of the Irish were blunted, that their health was affected and that they sought relief in their surroundings given to drinking and brawling. They remained long time victims of their circumstances, subject to the influences of their surroundings ... the instances of disorder and disturbance which occurred in the Irish quarter were the inevitable outcome of their situation.[32]

Problems of Acculturation

Conditions for the Irish were gradually improved from the late 1850s as a result of the increasing prosperity of the town and as the Irish adjusted to urban life. However, there is little evidence to suggest that the Irish as an ethnic group after a half-century and more of settlement in Leeds had been absorbed into the British way of life. As early as 1844, the slogan 'No Swaddy Irishmen or Soldiers Wanted Here' was inscribed on a table of The Green Man public house on York Street, close to both the Irish quarter and a large barracks. In 1866, there were rumours circulating around Leeds, which proved untrue, that the Irish were making pikes and drilling in secret in preparation for an uprising in the town that was to take place, rather predictably, on St Patrick's Day. These unfounded rumours proved premonitory: in February 1867 a large body of Irishmen left Leeds, Bradford, Halifax and Huddersfield evidently with the intention of joining with fellow Fenians in Chester to raid the castle's store of arms and ammunition. Police and troops were deployed in prospect of a disturbance. Meanwhile, in Leeds a young man carrying a parcel and acting suspiciously was approached and challenged by a constable. The parcel contained 24 packages containing 140 ball cartridges all greased and prepared for use. Later that same month packages of rifle cartridges were discovered in Morley railway tunnel.[33] In the December of 1867, following the execution of the Manchester Martyrs, large placards appeared all over Leeds:

GOD SAVE IRELAND

A funeral procession of the Irish patriots executed at Manchester on November 23rd 1867 will take place in Leeds on Sunday next, the 15th December. The procession will assemble at Vicar's croft, and start at two o'clock p.m., and will parade the principal streets to St Patrick's Cemetery, York Road. All lovers of Ireland, men and women, are requested to attend and show their respects to the memory of their fellow-countrymen.[34]

The Mayor of Leeds banned the procession, but Irish preparations for it continued. The authorities fearful of mass civil disobedience organised a major military security operation and consequently the procession never took place.

The media commented on the Irish presence in the crowds celebrating the visit of the Prince of Wales to Leeds in 1868:

Even the supposed Fenian sympathisers in Kirkgate... forgot to hiss. They cheered and cheered again – old hats that no-one but an Irishman would wear, brilliantly-coloured handkerchiefs

St Mary's Church from Tab Street, The Bank, c. 1900. Courtesy of Danny Kennally, Leeds Irish Historical & Cultural Society

'...migrant shops' (Cohen's & Kelly's), ...e Street, Leylands, 1901. Courtesy ...ds Library & Information Services

that only an Irish woman would delight in, were waved over and over again in the breeze, and the prince graciously and smiling acknowledged the greeting.[35]

The above wording would suggest that the Irishmen and Irishwomen were still considered alien, in dress at least, to the city's natives and that they could be distinctly picked out in a crowd. The Irish were also considered different in the minds of the working class; the British working class, Marx noted in 1870, 'feels himself a member of the ruling nation ... He cherishes religious, social and national prejudices against the Irish worker'.[36]

In 1870, H.M.I. Fitch gave an account of the lowest level of Irish emigrant residing in Leeds living a:

Life of indigence, squalor and hopelessness, which it is difficult for comfortable people to conceive. It is known that there are hundreds of families, whose average income from all sources does not exceed 1s per head per week ... There are rag-pickers, chip-sellers, and other persons of nondescript occupations; and there are hundreds of children in Leeds, the main preoccupations of whose life is to follow coal wagons about, with an old pail or basket.[37]

Table 1.1: Census of 1881: Inmates of Leeds Union Workhouse, Beckett Street

Birthplace of Inmates	Number of Inmates	As % of Total Inmates
England	328	73
Ireland	109	24
Scotland	8	1.6
Poland	1	0.2
Elsewhere	3	0.6
Total	449	100

Source: *Census of Population of England and Wales:* 1881, Enumerator's Returns

The British working class, Marx noted in 1870, 'feels himself a member of the ruling nation ... He cherishes religious, social and national prejudices against the Irish worker'.

The Irish situation in Leeds was little improved throughout the following decade. The 1881 census of England and Wales highlighted the fact that there was a disproportionate number of Irish relying on the town's workhouse for survival. Of the 449 inmates of the Leeds Union Workhouse on Beckett Street, 109 (58 male and 51 female) or 24 per cent were Irish-born (see Table 1.1). This same census recorded that the Irish constituted merely 3.1 per cent of the total population of Leeds borough. On closer inspection of the names and ages of the inmates it becomes clear that many more of those born in Leeds were of Irish blood. Many of the elderly men in the workhouse were recorded as bricklayer's, carpenter's or contractor's labourers, many of the elderly women as domestic servants or charwomen. Both men and women were also recorded as working as flax/cloth dressers or linen/stuff weavers. The men obviously were no longer in a capacity to fulfil the workload of such physically demanding positions and as the century progressed those involved in handloom weaving increasingly came under pressure since they could not compete with the power looms. It would appear that these Irish, more than 50 per cent of them then in the sixty to eighty age bracket, would have arrived during the famine decades and remained in the same occupations they initially secured without scaling the social or income ladders.

It would, however, appear that there were discernible differences within the Irish working classes in Leeds in the later Victorian period; Dillon remarks that:

There are sufficient examples ... to indicate that the Irish were not simply refugees from the famine. Taken alongside the evidence of continued immigration in the mid-50s, much of it still from Ireland, they add a further dimension to the story of Irish settlement. Leeds attracted the famine Irish, but it also attracted others, who were more capable of contributing to the well-being of the town upon arrival. Indeed, in 1860, the assistant overseer of the poor in Leeds reported that although the Irish were still arriving they were far more capable of looking after themselves than their predecessors of the late 1840s and early 1850'.[38]

Additionally, following the suppression of the procession in honour of the Manchester Martyr's the local press reported that 'in York Road very few people were assembled, but here some of the better class of Irish were walking about'.[39]

In 1895, the *Leeds Mercury* reported in a somewhat paranoid manner on an Irish Marian festival taking place in the city's suburb: 'as the procession wended its way along the principal streets, the Rosary was recited ... hymns ... sung, and we felt for the time being as if a sudden transformation into a Roman Catholic country had taken place'.[40] This astonishment at a celebration of faith by a community that had been residing in their midst for at least seventy years highlights the fact that there had been little interaction between the natives and the Irish emigrants. On occasion the reactions expressed in the local press appeared in the more serious form of religious bigotry and open hostility towards the Irish Catholics of Leeds:

In those days, the bigotry of the working class English made them [the Irish] cling together. The scoff and sneers had to be ignored as they set out for Sunday Mass. Bands of young Irish men had to walk together up the main road, the women kept together in the centre, to protect them from stones and blows that were hailed on them from bands of ignorant colliers, who resented the Irish Papists and stood in gangs to torment them as they went to church on Sundays.[41]

This sectarianism was on occasion was echoed in the mid-twentieth century.

By 1880 Irish immigration into Leeds had slowed and at the close of the century had virtually ceased, thus ending the first wave of Irish immigration into the town (see Table 1.2).

Table 1.2: Irish-born Population of Leeds*: 1841–1921

Census year	Irish-born Population	Total Population of Leeds	Irish-born as % of Total
1841	5,027	152,054	3.3
1851	8,466	172,270	4.9
1861	10,333	207,165	5.0
1871	10,128	259,212	3.9
1881	9,541	309,119	3.1
1891	7,166	367,505	2.0
1901	6,443	428,968	1.5
1911	4,739	454,155	1.0
1921	4,027	458,232	0.9

Source: *Census of Population of England and Wales*: 1841–1921, County Reports & Dillon, 'The Irish in Leeds, 1851-61'
*Note: Variously Borough, Urban Sanitary District, City & County Borough

In terms of numbers the only immigrant community to rival that of the Irish in Leeds in the nineteenth century was that of the Jews. Although there were Jews settling in Leeds from the 1750s, the traditional date for the foundation of the Jewish Community in Leeds is 1840. By 1851 the Leeds Jewish community numbered 144 persons, increasing to 988 persons in 1871 and to 7,856 in 1891. The Jews, like the Irish, settled in the heart of Leeds, in or near a dilapidated area of the town known as the Leylands. They, like the Irish, were predominantly working class and were met with much hostility; this hostility reached a climax in 1917 with a mob attack on the Leylands. In the late 1920s, the Leeds Jewish population peaked at around 22,000–25,000. If the Irish in Leeds were traditionally associated with labouring and millwork, then the Jews became synonymous with the cloth trade. By the late 1920s Burton's bespoke tailoring factory on Hudson Road, founded by a Lithuanian Jewish immigrant, was employing 16,000 and was the largest and most popular clothing store in Europe; by 1935 the majority of the 200 tailoring firms in Leeds were Jewish owned.[42]

> **If the Irish in Leeds were traditionally associated with labouring and millwork, then the Jews became synonymous with the cloth trade**

One marked difference between the Irish and Jewish communities is the relative speed with which, generally speaking, the Jewish community vacated their initial decrepit core area, scaled the economic ladder and moved to the plusher areas of Leeds. By the 1920s, the Jewish population were dispersing from the Leylands area, many moving to Chapeltown and Moortown. Today, 90 per cent of Leeds' Jews live in the prestigious Leeds 17 postal district (incorporating Alwoodley and Moor Allerton),[43] whereas the Irish are scattered across the city with minor concentrations in some inner-city wards, namely Harehills, Burmantofts, City and Holbeck, and Richmond Hill (see Table 1.4).

Development and Expansion of the Leeds Irish Community

The development and gradual spread of the initial Irish community and their descendants in Leeds may be tracked by analysing the successive establishment of Catholic parishes and churches in the city. According to Dr Bell, in his paper entitled 'Leeds: The Evolution of a Multi-Cultural Society', this process can be tracked in six phases of development,[44] three of which take place in the nineteenth century:

1. Initial Settlement Area: 1820–1830s
2. Great Famine Influx: 1840–1860s
3. Expansion: 1860s–1900
4. Pre-World War One: 1901–1914
5. Inter-war Spread to New Housing Estates: 1918–1939
6. Post-World War Two Expansion: 1945–1960s

Dr Bell suggests that the first phase of development included the establishment of St Patrick's Church and parish in the early 1830s and also the construction of St Anne's Catholic Church later that same decade. The second phase witnessed the establishment of Mount St Mary's on Richmond Hill in the Bank district of the town in 1857. This was followed by an extension south of the River Aire into the Hunslet district in which St Francis's became the parish church in 1860. In 1878 this initial grouping of parishes was combined to form the Catholic Diocese of Leeds.

During phase three, which took place between 1861 and 1901, Catholic churches and parishes were set up in Wortley (1872), Hyde Park (1891), Woodhouse (1891) and Beeston Hill (1896). This spread of the Irish population corresponded with the labour demands of the time, particularly that of the textile and engineering industries. A fourth phase of development, from 1901 to 1914, witnessed the establishment of Catholic churches and parishes in Beeston and Harehills, in and around developing working-class housing areas. The fifth phase, in the inter-war years but particularly in the 1930s, occurred hand-in-hand with the clearance of the slum dwellings of the in-township of Leeds and the energetic construction of thousands of new houses by the council for rent and sale. In the years following the First World War many Irish came to work on these building projects as the City Council, on the back of promises made by Prime Minister Lloyd George, strove to build suburban housing estates 'fit for heroes'. These estates include those at Crossgates, Osmondthorpe, Middleton and York Road and the private and council housing areas of Chapeltown, Bramley and Gipton. Today, the Beeston, Chapeltown, Gipton, Harehills, Hunslet and Woodhouse areas of Leeds are still home to significant Irish communities.

The sixth and final phase of Catholic parish expansion took place in the years following the end of the Second World War. The bulk of this spread was to the newly built housing areas of Seacroft and Swancliffe to the east, the Belle Isle estate to the South, Chapel Allerton and the Moortown estate to the north, Headingley, Spen Lane, the Ireland Wood estate and Cookridge to the north west, and in more recent times to the Cowclose estate and Stanningley to the west.

The Leeds Irish as a Community

Up to this point, the term 'community' has been used without definition to refer to the Irish in Leeds. However, 'community' is one of the most problematic terms in sociology in that it is vague, wide-ranging and largely without specific meaning. There are many ways in which to view a community, some of which are crude and exclusive, others of which are less tangible and more complex. A number of elements by which a community may be identified have been noted by King, Shuttleworth and Strachan;[45] these include:

1. Shared birthplace or shared ancestral origin
2. Geographical space
3. Creation and participation in various cultural/political/religious institutions
4. A common sense of identity and shared values
5. A social network of interacting individuals
6. The less tangible feeling of Irishness

Thus far 'Irish-born' has been used to refer to all those born on the island of Ireland, since in the nineteenth century and pre-1921 there was no border between north and south and therefore no distinction between those born in the six or twenty-six counties. Where the term 'Irish' has been used it has included Irish-born persons, their children and grandchildren. Identifying a community on the basis of shared birthplace or shared ancestral origin is crude and problematic because in many cases the individual may well not want to be or feel to be Irish or part of an Irish community. Significantly, whether or not

'Community' is one of the most problematic terms in sociology in that it is vague, wide-ranging and largely without specific meaning

the Irish viewed themselves or acted as a united community in nineteenth-century Leeds, the native English of the town certainly saw the Irish as a distinct and separate group.

The term community at the very least refers to a collection of people in a shared geographical area. The Irish formed a definite geographical community in mid-nineteenth-century Leeds, being concentrated in the in-township with a particularly high density in the Bank district, as a result of a number of factors. The development of steam-powered technology in the late eighteenth century encouraged the construction of textile factories in the East End of Leeds. To accommodate factory workers, farming land was purchased to the north east and south of the town and rows of back-to-back terraced houses were built. Conditions in and around the factories were crowded, sanitation and water supplies virtually non-existent and thus rent was cheap. The Irish came to settle in the Bank district in the 1820s and 1830s because rent was cheapest, factory employment was on the doorstep for man, woman and child and St Patrick's Catholic Church was nearby. The Bank was to retain a 'green tinge' for almost a century until the slum clearances of inner-city Leeds of the 1930s forced the relocation of the majority of its population to newer flats and houses. However, the Bank and its crowning edifice, Mount St Mary's Church, remains a symbol of the Irish community in Leeds. The Irish were not totally segregated from the native population; there were many native English working-class living in the same streets in the Bank. It is fair to assume that the Irish and their English neighbours intermingled but to what degree this took place is undeterminable, although it is known that some English families in the Bank converted to Catholicism.[46]

Another reason for the dense population in this area was the limited room for expansion; the area was bound to the south by the River Aire, to the north by the railway and York Road, to the east by the commercial town centre and to the west by open farmland. It would be fair to suggest that successive generations of Irish were attracted to the Bank not only because it was an established 'Irish quarter', but also due to the availability of cheap accommodation upon arrival and nearby employment opportunities, so enabling newcomers to avoid expensive public transport. It is also fair to assume that many were drawn to these areas populated by family, friends and neighbours where the inherent problems of settlement and dislocation from Irish society would have been eased in an environment of Irish character where accents were familiar and cultural practice was similar.

With regards to Irish institutions in Leeds, Mount St Mary's was built with the sweat and blood of the surrounding Irish community; some funds for the construction of the church were collected locally, but wealthy Catholics residing outside the area donated the bulk of money. The older St Patrick's Church further served the Irish community. However, it is estimated that in mid-nineteenth-century Britain 50 per cent of Irish emigrants permanently abandoned practicing Catholicism and the Irish of Leeds would have been no exception.[47]

Politically Irishmen such as Feargus O'Connor, Charles Connor and George White were all heavily involved in the Chartist movement in Leeds in the 1830s and 1840s and were involved in the physical force wing of the movement. In the late 1840s attempts were made to broaden the Chartist base in Leeds by attracting the town's Irish population but to what extent they were successful remains speculative. Before Daniel O'Connell had launched his 'monster-meeting' campaign for the restoration of political autonomy to Ireland in 1843, most large Yorkshire towns – Bradford, Dewsbury, Huddersfield, Leeds and Sheffield – had established Repeal Organisations. The Leeds Association had by 1843 opened five Repeal Reading Rooms and in nine months raised £80 towards the Repeal Rent.[48] In Leeds as elsewhere, the Catholic clergy were influential in persuading Irish emigrants and their families to enrol with O'Connell's Repeal movement.[49] There was also a Leeds Fenian Society; some Irish in nineteenth-century Leeds were involved in Fenian activity but it is likely that this was a small minority of the community. Nonetheless, with a sizeable Irish population in Leeds, the town's natives and authorities were nervous of a Fenian threat and tensions were high between the Irish and English communities.

An examination of Leeds directories from the 1880s onwards reveals the existence of numerous Irish clubs: The Irish National Club, 7 Trinity Street (later 165a, Briggate); The Irish National League Club, 40 Richmond Road; The United Irish Club, 40 Stillhouse Yard, Waterloo Road, Hunslet; The United Irish League Club, Gladstone Place, Wellington Road; The John Dillon United League Club of Great Britain, 2 Grimson Street; The United Irish National Club, 10 Musgreave's Fold, Bank; The Henry Grattan National Club, 2 Sowerby Street; and The Irish National Club (West Leeds Division), 56 Victoria Road.[50] Additionally, in the town there existed a Leeds Home Rule Association, which had its premises in Kirkgate. In 1883, the Irish National League for Great Britain was founded at a convention in Leeds; Charles Stuart Parnell headed the convention. In 1885 Parnell, the Irish Home Rule leader, urged Britain's Irish population to vote against Gladstone's Liberals. The Irish in the East Leeds constituency obliged and the Conservative candidate, R. Dawson, was subsequently elected. In the general election the following year Parnell transferred his support to the Liberals, after Gladstone had converted to Home Rule, and the only changed seat in Leeds was that of East Leeds.[51] Thus it would appear that there was a degree of political cohesion amongst the Irish population of Leeds; however, following the fall of Parnell the Irish community was split in its allegiance, the anti-Parnell faction went as far as to establish a separate Irish club.[52] The Irish National Club, which had been founded in the Bank, moved to premises situated off Lower Briggate at the close of the nineteenth century. In summary, if one is to look at the Irish in Leeds as a community through various cultural, political and religious institutions there is evidence that there was a degree of cohesion. However, there is no way of accurately estimating the numbers that ever joined these institutions or attended their gatherings; all that can be said with confidence is that each incorporated a fraction of the Leeds Irish community.

Mary J. Hickman advocates a sociological approach to the study of community that 'focuses on social relationships as the basis of 'community' rather than geographical space', which she argues 'is a more useful conception of community because ways of life do not necessarily coincide with settlement types'.[53] Ideally the analysis of social networks within a community would be preferential over a basic geographical study of a community; however, a difficulty arises in that there is no clear, widely accepted definition of just what characteristic features of social interaction constitute the relations typical of so-called communities.[54] In this regard oral history has been recognised as being 'most useful' in explaining the social structure and pattern of everyday life'.[55] However, for the Irish in nineteenth-century Leeds, this discipline evolved decades too late.

To what extent the Irish in Leeds in the nineteenth and early twentieth centuries interacted as a community during the course of their everyday lives is somewhat hazy. There is little documentary material which could shed light on the social relationships of the Irish in Leeds during this period. However, in *The Ham Shank*, Mary Patterson, in documenting the life of her Aunt Maggie (the daughter of a Mayo emigrant), sketches a picture of life in the Bank from the latter decades of the nineteenth century to its clearance in the 1930s. The narrative is particularly focused on religion but is also one of a humble existence with Irish emigrants 'living in the English way, but clinging fervently to their Irish customs, and above all to the Faith of their Fathers'.[56] She recalls that her aunt attended 'concerts given by the school children to celebrate the feast of St Patrick when the girls in their white dresses and emerald sashes and ribbons sang the Irish songs, and their parents proud and happy came along to applaud them'.[57] Patterson also alludes to the constant stream of young Irish emigrants to the Bank and religious tensions amongst the Irish and English.

One interesting point of note is that when Eamon de Valera escaped from Lincoln Jail in 1919, two of his fellow escapees, Sean McGarry and Sean Milroy, hid in the Bank within the Irish community for several days before returning to Ireland.[58] This would at the very least hint at a degree of social and political cohesion amongst the Irish in the district, in that fugitives could safely be accommodated amongst and within the community.

So did the Irish constitute a united community in nineteenth-century Leeds? The evidence suggests that in spatial terms they formed a distinct 'Irish Quarter' with offshoots. They were to be found in all eight wards of the township of Leeds but were for the most part residing in three wards, those of the East, the

Oral history has been recognised as being 'most useful' in explaining the social structure and pattern of everyday life

North and the North East. However, they were not segregated and dwelt amongst the English working class. They were almost exclusively Catholic, but not all were practicing Catholics, and politically it would seem that some were involved with the Fenians and the Home Rule movement. Little evidence remains concerning their cultural activities but there were Irish dances and St Patrick's Day celebrations in the town in the late 1800s. The Irish were also somewhat united in the fact that they were seen as outsiders by the native population and in many cases as a social problem and they were, almost without exception, working class. On the basis that the Irish were of a shared birthplace or ancestry, that they were residing in numbers in a definable area, that the majority were working class and of the one religion, that they could be called upon to unite in times of difficulty (for the procession for the Manchester Martyrs and by Parnell to unite the Irish vote) one would have to view the Irish in Leeds as a community united to varying degrees. The Irish in Ireland were not a homogeneous group and neither were its emigrant sons and daughters living abroad.

To summarise, the story of the Irish in nineteenth-century Leeds is, in many respects, similar to that of the Irish in many of Britain's urban centres during this period. By the 1820s Leeds had a small Irish population, which had arrived most likely via the port of Liverpool and which was attracted by employment opportunities in the textile industry and in the construction of housing, railways and canals. They initially took root in the East End of Leeds, the most impoverished working-class area of the town around the mills and factories, where housing was cheapest. Increased native population movement into Leeds from the countryside coincided with the continued arrival of Irish emigrants in the 1830s. This rapid influx and sustained urban growth added further strain to the already inadequate conditions of the working class. Thus the town of Leeds was ill-prepared for the sheer numbers of destitute Irish who arrived in the latter years of the 1840s. Conditions worsened in the East End of Leeds, cholera and typhus spread rapidly into adjoining quarters and the town struggled to come to terms with the increased strain on its resources. The Famine Irish bore the brunt of the blame for the desperate social conditions; however, these conditions existed not only in Leeds but also in almost all contemporary major industrial centres throughout Britain and were mostly the result of rapid industrial expansion. A number of reports on the social conditions of the working class in Britain, which were carried out in the years before the famine influx (early 1840s), indicates that there were universal housing and sanitation problems as a result of the Industrial Revolution.[59] The desperate situation was not caused but *was* compounded by the influx of the Famine Irish in Leeds. As the century wore on the Irish in Leeds were still for the most part located within the initial core settlement area and were over-represented in the poverty and crime statistics of Leeds. They suffered from bad press and on occasion open hostility from their fellow working-class neighbours as religious differences and competition for employment strained community relations. Thus the Irish formed a distinct geographical, spiritual and social community. The Leeds Fenian Society had been involved in an abortive attack on Chester Castle in 1867 and a funeral procession organised in the town 'in honour of the Irish patriots executed at Manchester' met with strong military and police resistance. Gradually the Irish in Leeds began to adopt more constitutional methods to achieve their political aims and the working-class area of East Leeds became a constituency decided by the Irish vote.[60] The Irish had begun to organise themselves as an ethnic group at the end of the nineteenth century; the Irish National Club had been established in the Bank and by the 1890s had moved to Trinity Street, off Lower Briggate Street. Evidence suggests that at the close of the century the Irish were still visibly different from the native population in their politics, dress, religion and culture. It is difficult to estimate how in terms of social interaction, recreational activity, cultural tradition (other than religion) and community aspirations the Irish differed as an ethnic grouping from the native population in nineteenth-century Leeds. The only accounts which survive were written from outside the community and focus upon the negative aspects of the Irish population of Leeds – their squalid living conditions, their poor state of health, the criminal activity of a minority of its members, etc. With regards to their hopes and desires, their daily lives and recreational activities, no record survives. Oral history would have been an ideal instrument by which such information could have been elicited and recorded for posterity; however, it remains forever lost.

Quarry Hill flats, 1946.
Courtesy of Leeds Library
& Information Services

Quarry Hill flats, 1951.
Courtesy of Leeds Library
& Information Services

The Irish in Leeds Post-1931

The Irish-born population of Britain declined in the early decades of the twentieth century, in both absolute and relative terms.[61] The establishment of the Irish Free State in 1921 failed to initiate a mass return of Irish emigrants from Britain. From the 1930s Britain took the place of the United States as the choice of destination favoured by Irish emigrants; this occurred as a result of depression in the US, the imposition of immigration quotas by Congress and the difficulties in transatlantic travel during the Second World War. This second wave of large-scale emigration from Ireland to Britain took place between the mid-1930s and the early years of the 1970s. This began as a trickle in the 1920s, gradually increased during the 1930s, gathering momentum during the war years and in the post-war reconstruction of Britain. By 1931 the Irish-born population of England and Wales had fallen to 381,089 (0.9 per cent of the total population). As a result of the surge of emigration in response to the intense demand for labour in war and post-war Britain the Irish-born population of England and Wales rose to 870,445 in 1961, peaking at 878,530 (1.9 per cent of the total population) in 1966.

Table 1.3: Irish-born Population of Leeds (County Borough): 1931–1981

Census year	Irish-born Population	Total Population of Leeds	Irish-born as % of Total
1931	3,165	482,809	0.66
1941	No Census	No Census	No Census
1951	4,788	505,219	0.95
1961	6,632	510,676	1.30
1971	7,580	496,010	1.53
1981*	7,563	696,714	1.09

Source: *Census of Population of England and Wales*: 1921–1981, County Reports

Note: * These figures are for Leeds Metropolitan District and not Leeds Borough

The 1930s and 1940s

By 1931 the Leeds Irish-born population had fallen to 3,165, its lowest figure for a century (Tables 1.2 and 1.3). By the 1920s, Leeds' textile industry was in decline and tailoring and manufacturing became the dominant industries. Unemployment in Leeds was high in the 1920s and 1930s.[62] However, in the 1930s many Irishmen in the city secured work in industries with a long tradition of employing Irish labour, notably the building trade. The largest public housing scheme in Europe, the Quarry Hill flats ranging from four to eight storeys high and comprising 938 flats for over 3,000 people on a 26-acre site, was begun in 1934. Built on the former site of the city's most notorious Victorian slums, the state-of-the-art complex incorporated lifts and an automatic waste disposal system which channelled domestic refuse and sink waste directly from the flats to central incinerators. This complex was home to many Irish families in the 1950s and 1960s.

It was all navvy work; it was all buildings then; there was building going on at the time. Now it [unemployment] was very bad up to the end of 1938 when the war clouds ... then things began to brisk up because they knew there was war coming. Now prior to that when I went there first you'd see notices up in factories 'No Irish Need Apply' and then all of a sudden that changed to 'Irishmen Wanted'. They wanted ya, not just in there at the factory, they wanted ya, what meant by that was they wanted ya in the army. You went for a job then they'd say 'Well, we only take certain aged men in here, what age are ya? Alright, well you're eligible for the army'. [Austin, b. 1916, Co. Roscommon]

Many more Irishmen were employed in the agricultural sector around Yorkshire. Of their female counterparts many found work as domestics, in the services or in the thriving clothing trade. Leeds of the 1930s was still a heavily industrialised and consequently a filthy city in the eyes of its new Irish arrivals:

I hated it, I detested it, them days there was no such thing as a blue sky, it was black with soot and muck, even the footpaths were black with muck, the walls were black with muck, it was a terrible, it was, what do you call, an industrial city, and I couldn't understand why it was so black. [Eileen, b. 1918, Co. Mayo]

Leeds had a relatively sizeable Mayo contingency in the post-famine decades and by 1930s it was fast becoming established as a 'Mayo town'.[63] One Galway woman recalls of the Irish in Leeds in the late 1930s that 'every single one was from Mayo and they all went to St Francis'. St Francis's was an Irish social club organised by the Catholic clergy and well known throughout Yorkshire and in Ireland. There weren't many Irish owned or Irish managed pubs in 1930s Leeds, but Austin remembers that two pubs, The Simpson Arms, on York Road, and The (old) Roscoe, in Sheepscar, were frequented by the Irish. One Mayo veteran described his memories of being Irish in 1930s Leeds:

We were all very sensitive and unsure then. We'd cling together a lot with lads from our own county. After Mass we'd go to a pub in Leeds frequented by Mayo men. The talk would be mostly about Mayo and who was doing what back there – or about Mayo men here, or what they were doing in the 'diggin's'. After that we might have a meal, but never in a place that looked 'proper', with tablecloths and so on. We'd be scared to go into a place like that, even on Sunday with our best suits on, in case they'd throw us out for not knowing how to behave properly at table. We all shared rooms in digs, and sometimes we shared beds – but no immorality mind you – and sent money home most weeks and said we were getting on fine at the buildin' – even though in the thirties we'd have work only about three weeks out of four. When you met someone you knew, the remark was always 'Are ye workin'?' It was up to yourself to get work when it was scarce, by letting on to a foreman what a great worker you could be if you were given a job. Some fellows used to develop a particular way of walking – they called it 'The Gimp' – it amounted to a sort of swagger which gave an impression of confidence. When a fellow with 'The Gimp' came onto a site, he'd kick any ould timber out of his way – fuck it outa his way, as much as to say:

Leeds had a relatively sizeable Mayo contingency in the post-famine decades and by 1930s it was fast becoming established as a 'Mayo town'.

'You want a tunnel dug ... I'll dig it myself in a day.' And then coming to England with the lads and sticking together, being afraid to talk to English girls, and all the time this brooding thing of history ... well it didn't help you in so-called integrating.[64]

The description is one of Irish youths lacking in self-confidence, living in cramped conditions, without constant employment but sending money home under the pretence that all was well and finding comfort and solace amongst their own.

The reception of the Irish emigrants in Britain was not always amicable. On 16 January 1939 there were three IRA explosions in Manchester; one person was killed. Mass arrests followed the attacks but the campaign continued with further bomb outrages in Birmingham, Cardiff, Coventry, Derby, Leicester and Liverpool; train stations, banks, post offices, bridges and pylons were the prime targets of over 200 explosions. The IRA campaign peaked with the killing of five people in an explosion in Coventry on 25 August, eight days before the outbreak of the Second World War. For the most part Yorkshire escaped the IRA's campaign of terror; however, in July 1939 Belfast-born James McGowan was, with four others, arrested after 20 lbs of gelignite was discovered at a house in Potternewton, Leeds. In November, at the Leeds Assizes, McGowan was given a twelve-year sentence; the others were not proceeded against.[65] The British government swiftly responded to such attacks by introducing the Prevention of Violence Bill in July 1939, which required all Irishmen in Britain to register with the police. Thus, perhaps understandably, Irish emigrants were often treated with suspicion, mistrust and on occasion open hostility, a situation which lasted well into the 1950s. The immediate result was the reluctance to employ the Irish and the difficulty in securing 'digs'.

On 1 and 2 September 1939, 18,000 children, 2,800, teachers and 8,000 mothers were evacuated from Leeds, mostly to Lincolnshire and the Yorkshire Dales. However, some Irish parents decided to send their children to the relative safety of the west of Ireland and took part in the war effort:

When he [husband] went into the army and the two kids went (sic) evacuated home to Ireland to me mothers, I went into munitions ... I worked two-and-a-half years doin' a man's work ... in the munitions and it was like being in the army, you had to do it, you couldn't say no, it was the women that made all them munitions to keep the men in the field. [Honora, b. 1914, Co. Galway]

When, in September 1939, the war broke out many Irish in Leeds decided to return to Ireland because of conscription into the British forces and the fear of the inevitable bombings:

When the war broke out we came home to Mayo; I didn't want to but my sister was afraid we'd be bombed in our beds. [Bridget, b. 1918, Co. Mayo]

Oh I decided that I wasn't goin' to fight for England anyway, I'll be straight about that, and I often told them that too. But I decided then that the best thing to do was to keep an eye out to see how near it was coming and to get out of there before it would come, the trouble you know so ... me wife came home first ... she came back to her parents' place and I stayed there a while to put a few quid together ... I was asked to join the air force, you know, it was recommended to ya to join the air force ... if you went into we'll say a labour exchange now, that's the first thing that they'd want ya to sign on for the ... in the forces, you know. Everywhere you went that was it 'Join the British Army, Join the British Air Force'. [Austin, b. 1916, Co. Roscommon]

However, many others decided to stay, some to protect their new lives and homes:

I couldn't go home, I was living in Leeds and I had to stand me ground in Leeds because our home was there; we had got a house. But I went home for our Gareth to be born but I came back again. And father [her husband] **of course was in tailoring and then he was taken into the army and then I couldn't** [return to Ireland] **because we had the children to think of to come back. That was our home; we had given up everything at home.** [Honora, b. 1914, Co. Galway]

It is estimated that around 100,000 men and 10,000 women from Leeds registered for service, of which the city's Irish community contributed a share. Since there was no census taken in 1941 it is impossible to estimate with any certainty the Irish-born population of Leeds during the war years, and besides many more moved eastwards across the Irish Sea as the demand for war-time labour intensified.

The fear of bombing proved founded and 1940 witnessed the first air raid by the German Luftwaffe on Leeds. In the following year, on the night of 14 March, the German Luftwaffe damaged 4,600 houses, the museum and the Town Hall; 65 people were killed and a further 260 injured, 56 seriously. The raid is vividly recalled by one Irish emigrant:

One night these German planes come over and the search lights was on, well they come this way and you could see the swastikas on them and they let one of the fire bombs fall down on the yard ... and we had sandbags at the time and I picked up one of them and I said to my husband 'put it out quick or we'll be all [dead]**.' So the next street there was two back-to-back houses blown up.** [Honora, b. 1914, Co. Galway]

On 8 May 1945 Victory parties were held on the streets of Leeds. The city's final war damage statistics: 77 civilian dead, 327 injured and 197 buildings destroyed with a further 7,623 damaged in 9 air raid attacks. However, material damage to Leeds was minimal in comparison with other cities such as Birmingham, Coventry, Hull, Liverpool, London and Sheffield.[66]

As elsewhere in Britain, the post-war prosperity experienced by Leeds resulted in a shortfall of labour in the lower-paid jobs such as in the hospitals or on the buses. Furthermore, mass cheap manual labour was required in the post-war reconstruction of Britain. For example, in 1948 it is estimated that there were 90,000 substandard houses unfit for human habitation in Leeds, of which 56,000 were back-to-backs, out of a total of 154,000.[67] Thus new estates were sited near the city centre and around the Outer Ring Road. By the late 1940s, Britain increasingly turned to the colonies in the Caribbean to satiate this demand for labour. However, the Irish, Britain's traditional supplier of cheap labour, remained the largest immigrant group in Leeds and in Britain in general with an average annual net migration of 24,384 persons from Ireland for the post-war period of 1946-51.[68] In 1948, the Yorkshire County Board, the governing body of Gaelic Football, was established; Canon Stritch was the board's first chairman.

The 1950s and 1960s

The 1951 census revealed that there were 4,788 Irish-born persons residing in Leeds, an increase of 1,632 in the previous two decades, and the population of Leeds borough for the first time broke the half-million mark. The ethnic mix of Leeds was further added to during the 1950s and 1960s as large numbers from the West Indies and the Indian Subcontinent arrived in the city. They for the most part settled in the inner-city wards where rent was cheapest and conditions were worst. Much of this Irish population came to reside in the streets in and around the Chapeltown, Sheepscar and Harehills districts, to the north-east of the city centre. Economically Leeds was notably prosperous in the 1950s, 1960s and 1970s. As a result of this economic boom, the Leeds Irish population surged by almost 2,000 persons during the 1950s

Leeds Fleadh Cheoil, Primrose
Hill School, 1971. Courtesy of
Maureen Dwyer Ferguson. Top

Three hand reel, Irish National Club,
Lower Briggate, 1967. Ferguson/
McGowan Archive. Above left

Ferguson 'sisters', Irish National Club,
Lower Briggate, 1967. Ferguson/
McGowan Archive. Above right

Opening of Leeds Irish Centre, York
Road, 1970. Courtesy of Leeds
Library & Information Services. Left

and by a further 1,000 in the 1960s, peaking at 7,580 in 1971 (see Table 1.3). This surge resulted in greater needs for the Leeds Irish community, better sports and social facilities were required and also a social services department to provide advice to new arrivals on housing and employment. In 1967, the *Yorkshire Evening Post* revealed plans for a new Irish Centre to be built on a three-acre site off York Road at an estimated cost of £120,000; the leasehold on the Irish National Club off Lower Briggate was to expire in September 1969. In the report Mr Patrick Kissane, the then secretary of the club, estimated the city's Irish community at about 45,000, of which 16,000 were Irish-born and the remainder of Irish parentage.[69] This overestimation was highlighted in the 1971 census, which gave an Irish-born figure of less than 7,000 for Leeds (and a Northern Irish-born figure of less than 3,000). The proposed Irish Centre was to consist of a licensed club premises, a dancehall, sports fields and other social facilities. Funds for the centre were to be sought from industrial and commercial organisations in Ireland and also from the Roman Catholic Diocese of Leeds. In July 1969, at a meeting in Birmingham of the Council of Britain, permission was granted for a Comhaltas Ceoltóirí Éireann (CCÉ) branch to be formed in Leeds.

The 1970s

In terms of population, the census of 1971 recorded 33,310 people residing in the city of Leeds born outside of the United Kingdom, of which 6,565 were born in the Republic of Ireland. Moreover, 2,715 were born in Northern Ireland and a further 1,015 born in Ireland did not indicate a specific location. As has been discussed in the previous chapter this latter figure may be added to the figure for those born in the Republic of Ireland with a degree of confidence that the majority were born there. In addition to this these figures, there are many more second, and even third-generation Irish, although precise figures are lacking, who are conscious of and reflect their Irish cultural background.

The 1970s' construction of the M1 and M62 motorways, at a time when the use of the canals and railway had faded, further provided Irish labourers with seemingly never-ending work and reinforced Leeds' importance as a commercial centre, the crossroads of the north–south and east–west highways.

The Leeds Irish Centre was officially opened on 8 June 1970 replacing the older Irish National Club off Lower Briggate. Also in 1970, Leeds CCÉ was invited by BBC Radio Leeds to broadcast a fortnightly programme of traditional Irish music and song. In May 1972, the Leeds CCÉ hosted Fleadh Cheoil na Breataine at Primrose Hill Secondary School, which also served as the location for the Annual Leeds Fleadh Cheoil. In 1973, the Leeds CCÉ launched a branch magazine entitled *A Chara*, in which members penned articles, anecdotes and poems celebrating Irish culture and tradition. In January 1980, Radio Leeds became the first radio station in Britain to broadcast a show exclusively devoted to traditional Irish music; the programme entitled 'If You're Irish' survived for eight years.

Interestingly in 1982 the *Catholic Leeds Diocesan Directory* gave a population of the Leeds Catholic parishes of 52,380 persons. It has been noted that 'as a general estimate it has been said that 80 per cent of Catholics are of Irish descent in three generations. This would give a population of Irish origin in

Leeds of more than 40,000'.[70] This, of course, does not take into account those of the Irish Protestant community who have emigrated to Leeds, or indeed those who entered into mixed marriages.

Table 1.4: Leeds Wards with the Highest Concentration of Irish-born in 1981

Leeds Ward	Irish-born as % of Total Irish Population of Leeds
Harehills	10.67
Chapel Allerton	06.22
Burmantofts	05.79
Kirkstall	05.39
City and Holbeck	04.84
Richmond Hill	04.54
Headingley	04.43
Armley	03.99
Seacroft	03.29
Wortley	03.01

Source: *Census of Population of England and Wales*: 1981

In 1981 the Irish-born population of Leeds was distributed across the thirty-three wards of Leeds. Of the 7,563 Irish-born persons residing in Leeds in 1981 57 per cent were to be found in the eleven wards listed above (see Table 1.4) which are located, in part or entirely, in Urban Priority Areas; the remaining 43 per cent were scattered amongst the remaining twenty-two wards. At present according to the Index of Local Deprivation two of the above wards, those of Harehills and City and Holbeck, which together contain 15.5 per cent of Leeds' Irish-born population, are amongst the top 100 most deprived wards in England; there are 3,619 wards in England.

Leeds Irish Community, 1931–81

As aforementioned the development of Leeds' Irish community can be tracked by analysing the establishment of successive new Catholic parishes and churches in the city. Additionally, respondents' reminiscences provide an insight into the city's Irish community. Interestingly, one respondent believed the Irish community in Leeds was more readily apparent through a network of church, pub and work than in terms of a particular geographical area:

There was a feeling in the 50s anyway that I seem to recall of the Irish sticking very much together particularly in matters of work, you know a lot of them worked in the construction industry and they more or less dominated that, it was kinda like an Irish mafia you know in the building trade. There was that kind of thing and you know they did of course concentrate in the pubs you know so there was that kind of a thing you know, the community, if you like, was in the church and the pubs and in work more than anything else, you know, that's my memory of it anyhow. [Thomas, b. 1941, Dublin]

The majority of the respondents identified the Irish community with particular areas of the city. It has been noted that the Bank was the Irish stronghold for almost a century until the slum clearances in the 1930s scattered its Irish population. Information gleaned from the oral history interviews confirms that from the late 1940s to the 1970s the Irish population was most heavily concentrated on and off York Road and in the Burmantofts, Chapeltown, Harehills and Sheepscar districts and particularly around Chapeltown Road, Roundhay Road and Harehills Lane. These were Jewish areas in the opening decades of the twentieth century but as that community prospered it gradually moved northwards from the Leylands to Sheepscar, and since the Second World War via Chapeltown, Moortown and Roundhay to Alwoodley.[71]

I remember the Jews coming and settling in Leeds in the old days, Claypit Lane [the Leylands] they were all, and Spencer Place [Chapeltown]... well that was the top grade, all Jewish doctors and specialists they all lived in Spencer Place... and the Jews had their own hospital there, they had their own Jewish hospital, nearly all the big doctors and them in Leeds they were all Jewish. Well the Jews ran Leeds, let's put it this way. [Honora, b. 1914, Co. Galway]

Other significant Irish clusters were to be found to the north-west of the city in Headingley and south of the River Aire in Beeston and Hunslet, particularly around Dewsbury Road. However, by general consensus Harehills and the neighbouring Chapeltown emerged as being *the* focal point of the Irish community from the late 1940s to the 1970s. One contributor to the Leeds Comhaltas commemorative magazine in 1989, on the occasion of their twentieth anniversary, recalled of the Irish community in Leeds in the early 1950s that:

Anybody who lived in Chapeltown in those days could say they lived in Ireland. If you walked into Potternewton Park on a Sunday you would have thought you were in St Stephen's Green in Dublin. Irish boys and girls in their hundreds, hurlers and footballers, and somewhere under a tree the occasional sound of the accordion, fiddle and flute. Then there was Reginald Terrace a hundred yards from the park. Surely this should be called Patrick Street or Irish Town. Three houses stand out in my mind, numbers 19, 21 and 23, to be joined in 1951 by numbers 25 and 31 ... Well with five houses and about a hundred boys and girls it means a lot of birthday parties in a year. As a matter of fact I'm sure it was non-stop partying. The Irish music and dancing was all the go. I think that every musician that ever came to Leeds played in 23 Reginald Terrace ... Then there was week-end dancing at places such as St Francis' on Saturday night and the Holy Rosary on Sunday afternoon (and Sunday night in later years), also Claypit Lane and the Green Rooms.[72]

Harehills and the neighbouring Chapeltown emerged as being the focal point of the Irish community from the late 1940s to the 1970s.

Spencer Place, Gipton Street, Chapeltown, 1950. Courtesy of Leeds Library & information Services. Above.

Reginald Terrace (or 'Patrick Street'), Chapeltown, c. 1950. Courtesy of Leeds Library & Information Services. Top left.

Back to back housing in Bayswater Avenue. Courtesy of Leeds Library & Information Services. Left.

Terraced housing, Harehills, 1950. Courtesy of Leeds Library & Information Services. Below left.

Gráinne recalled the continued Irish predominance of this area in the 1960s:

There was a lot of Irish [in Leeds] **and they all lived down Harehills Road, near St Augustine's Church, that was all the Irish community, if ever you came to Leeds and you wanted to find somebody Irish you came there. And there used to be a park called Potternewton Park and we all met there on a Sunday. Now a white person daren't walk through there** [laughs] **so it changed so much. But all the Irish were brilliant, everybody sort of knew everybody an' stuck up for each other and helped and what have ya. And then that place started going down and they started moving out to the outskirts of Leeds and scattered all over, so you lost contact with a lot of them; the only time you meet people now is when it's at a funeral, that's mostly when you meet them all. It is, it's awful, it really is.** [Gráinne, b. 1945, Co. Mayo]

Michael, the son of Mayo emigrants, was born and raised in Harehills and recalls that it was easy to believe that this area was the only Irish enclave in the city during the 1950 and 1960s:

You see I only knew about Harehills at that time and I thought that all the Irish in Leeds [were] in Harehills but I found out afterwards that there was a lot out in Dewsbury Road [South Leeds] **as well, a lot of Irish living out there.** [Michael, b. 1947, Leeds]

Of the south Leeds area Liam recalls that when he first lived in Beeston:

There were very few [Irish in Beeston]**, but then about the fifties you started getting a lot of them in you know and nearly every one of 'em were from Mayo, nearly every one. Because they used to run a dance down at St Francis' which is not there now and you'd go in there on a Saturday night and it were all the culchies and they were all very clique you know.** [Liam, b. 1934, Co. Wexford]

Liam also provides a reason why those living in the Harehills area might not be very aware of the Irish in south Leeds:

We lived in Beeston, and Beeston was full of Irish but very rare you used to get them coming over to the club [Leeds Irish Centre] **you know they all used to have there own one pub in Beeston that nearly all the Irish went to. At one time there was three pubs up there with Irish landlords in 'em and we all used to use them you know. The only time you used to go up the Irish Centre was** [for example when] **one of my biggest mates ... Mick lost his wife and she was young you know was Kathy, she died young and left five kids an' we used the Irish Centre for a charity, well they used to do charity dances then, whatever come in used to go to Mick for the family.** [Liam, b. 1934, Co. Wexford]

Michael's sister added that the Irish community of Dewsbury Road consisted of many emigrants from the Killala and Lacken areas of North Mayo whereas the Harehills area had a greater concentration from the Attymass, Ballina, Charlestown, Swinford and Foxford region. This suggests that not only were emigrants attracted to the city by family and friends but also to certain areas within the city in which people from within their towns and parishes had settled.

In Harehills and Chapeltown Irish families bought or rented whole houses and occasionally they in turn sub-let rooms to single emigrants. Single Irishmen, either unmarried or with a wife in Ireland, often rented houses together. There were also many 'digs' style accommodations run by native and Irish landladies, many of which were situated around Spencer Place and off Roundhay Road. These were formerly the grand and spacious houses of the Jewish community, which because of their large rooms suited sub-division to cope with the housing needs of Irish emigrants into the area. Although Harehills and Chapeltown are remembered as the core of the Irish community in Leeds during this period that is not to suggest that the Irish outnumbered the native population in these areas. In fact, there may have been only a handful of houses in which Irish emigrants were residing on any one of the hundreds of streets that made up these areas. Generally speaking the standard of housing in Harehills was superior to that of Chapeltown throughout this period; in the 1950s Chapeltown contained mainly back-to-backs and houses divided into flats whereas Harehills was mainly comprised of terraced houses. The Holy Rosary Church served the Catholic congregation of Chapeltown and St Augustine's Church served that of Harehills. Thomas, who moved from Dublin to Leeds as a young teenager, arrived in Chapeltown in 1955:

He [Thomas's father] found us a flat in a pretty rough area of Leeds – Chapeltown, which was an area of once former splendour, big Victorian houses but in the fifties they'd gone down, they were just the worst flats for people, you know, whereas they were originally built as single family houses. And we lived there for a couple of years and we got moved to a council estate, an area called Meanwood and we lived there for...well up until the day I got married in 1978 we lived there. And my parents that's where they basically lived and died.

BMcG: And were there many Irish living in the area when you moved to Chapeltown?

In Chapeltown there was at that time in the fifties, not so much now, over the course of the years more and more Black and Asian emigrants came into the area and the Irish gradually moved out. It was also a Jewish area Chapeltown, most of the small shops and that were owned by Jews but it's all changed, it's predominantly an Afro-Caribbean neighbourhood now you know. The real Irish area, the old Leeds Irish area was an area called the Bank, yeah? But I've no experience of that, we didn't live there. But there was, long after the Irish kinda basically moved out of Chapeltown, I don't mean everyone of them moved out there was of course still some of them there, but it was no longer what you'd call an Irish area but some of the pubs remained Irish, like The Roscoe and The Pointers, The Victoria, The Regent, they are all more or less in that area you know and they still remained Irish and still do to this day.

BMcG: When you came here first, where were the main Irish concentrations in the city?

Well there was quite a few around Chapeltown. The Bank, that got pulled down in the fifties but I'm not sure when in the fifties, there was a lot of Irish people lived up the York Road area and down around Sheepscar which is very close to Chapeltown anyway. A lot of the old Irish from the Bank got moved up to new, new-ish housing estates like Halton and Seacroft and places like that, you know, so they're more scattered now. There's no real one Irish area, there isn't one area you could say is definitely Irish now. They're spread and integrated all over the city, you know. So I was never conscious of living in a definite Irish area as such, it was very much a mixed area was Chapeltown anyway, you know there was an Irish community, but there was also a Polish community, a Jewish community and so on. [Thomas, b. 1941, Dublin]

Evidence suggests that rather than being an Irish area, Sheepscar and Chapeltown in the 1950s and 1960s were areas where many of the city's immigrant population resided: Polish, Jews, Black and Irish (alongside the native population). It would appear that Harehills was a more exclusive area than Chapeltown at this time.

By all accounts there was a vibrant Irish social scene in Leeds in the 1950s and 1960s. The respondents gave the impression that this era was the heyday of the Leeds Irish community. This was perhaps due to the fact that the city's Irish population had increased, work was plentiful and consequently the emigrants found themselves with more disposable income than they were used to. Leeds it seems was a Mecca for Irish emigrants, with St Francis's Social Club, Holbeck, and The Shamrock Dancehall, Kirkgate, to which Irish revellers came from all over Yorkshire:

In them days [early 1960s] there used to be a coach that would come in from, start in Halifax, call to Huddersfield, then into Bradford, and to Brighouse and then into Leeds because all those places they had no dancehalls of their own once you see, so they all used to come into Leeds for the, you know, there used to be two or three coaches come like into Leeds on a Saturday and Sunday night you see. [Martin, b. 1940, Co. Mayo]

Martha and Martin recall of The Shamrock Dancehall:

Oh it was terrific, we used to go three nights a week to it, and walk home, we used to walk, there was tram lines on North Street when we first came and we'd walk home at night, there was a bus for Briggate but by the time we all come out and talk, all the gang, you'd just walk home, and you'd walk in your bare feet because you'd be wearing those stupid stiletto heels and your feet would be crippled dancing all night so you'd just come out take them off an' walk in your bare feet home and we thought nothing of it, nothing. It wouldn't take us long. And then we'd all stand talking because there's be people going in different directions because everybody went up to Harehills then, that's where everybody lived, or Beeston or Harehills ... and there used to be a coffee bar there at Spencer Place, the Rendezvous, an' we'd go in there for coffees. Well he [husband] didn't drink, he was a pioneer for years so he never took a drink so we sort of went to pictures and different things, he wasn't into drink, we'd go up to Roundhay Park and out on the boats when they'd go to the pubs. [Martha, b. 1946, Co. Longford]

I met my wife Marian in 1962, in early sixty-two ... in the dancehall the Shamrock it was and ... I asked her for a dance, you know like, and she said 'oh yes' like you know, so we were out on the floor and dancing around so then like after the three bars, you know, when you're chatting somebody you say the usual craic was them days "will you come for a mineral" ...there was no beer bar, there was all a mineral bar or a tea bar you know like. Do you want to go for a mineral you know like you thought that was the half-way house [laughs], you knew if you could get them for a mineral like you could get a start working on them more like ya know. [Martin, b. 1940, Co. Mayo]

The fact that the two primary Irish dancehalls did not serve alcohol does not mean that the nights were alcohol free as the evening usually began in one of the city's many Irish pubs. In response to the demand created by the numbers of young Irishmen pouring into Leeds, Irish landlords began to take over a number of public houses throughout the city. There was a particular concentration of Irish drinking establishments in the Sheepscar, Chapeltown, Harehills and Burmantofts areas of the city; The Regent, The Roscoe (old and new), The Pointer's, The Queen's, The Victoria, The Golden Lion, The Prince Arthur, The Eagle, The Harp, The Skinner's, The Fountain, The Woodpecker, Delaney's and The Ceilidh House were all at one time or another managed by Irish landlords. In Leeds city centre The Royal Oak, The Wellington, The Market Tavern and The Golden Cock were also at various times Irish run. In the Hyde Park area The Masons, The Coburg and The Fenton were 'Irish pubs', as were The Vic, The Black Bull and The Gardener's in Hunslett.

They all wore suits, they all wore ties, they all wore wide trousers like that, most of them at that time wore hats, in the late fifties, and they all had a certain gait about them, this kinda ... but it was very pronounced, I mean ya won't see it, see it with Irish fellas round here now, you won't see it in England as much but I mean with their hands in their pocket and them coming down the road it was a really pronounced, not exaggerated, down the road and everybody would be walking the same way. I used to think when I was getting a bit older into me late teens that it was the type of work people did with over the years at home or abroad, I don't know what it was really, so you picked somebody out an' they had kinda dark hair, black hair mostly and they had ruddy complexions so you could see Irish people ... I used to notice them particularly because they'd be in twos an' threes an' fours on a Sunday comin' or goin' to Mass or goin' down to the pubs, down Roundhay Road, there'd be streams of people walking like that down Roundhay Road in that type of dress...well when you went down Roundhay Road from Harehills where you met The Pointers, The Vic, The Prince of Wales, The Roscoe, The Regent, all the pubs were in a kind o' a round long bend there altogether and because they were all heading off to the pub on a Sunday. [Michael, b. 1947, Leeds]

These pubs and clubs were much more than just places to frequent at the weekend; they represented familiarity in the urban unknown. Together they constituted a vital network of friendly faces and accents, where information about work and lodgings could be shared. Poet Pearse Hutchinson who spent an evening in The Regent in the 1970s, which was then managed by a couple from Co. Mayo, penned the following lines:

> In the Regent in Leeds therewas just one lonely Englishman; bar us. Lemonade was the strongest Cathal would take but he had Planxty Johnson for ever, Liam Óg was there and Sligomen in town, and others making music besides them and others drinking and all of us gulping down the music, I said to Francie in the jax 'Here we are,' and he took the words right out of my mouth 'in the heart of England' – 'in the heart of Ireland' said I correcting him.[73]

His words explain why the Irish pub became a central institution for the Irish in Britain: the emigrant could forget or at least ignore for a time that he was away from home. Michael, however, recalls that the role of the Irish pubs in Leeds changed somewhat from 1970 following the opening of the new Irish Centre on York Road:

Thing[s] changed in 1970 when the Irish Centre came in because prior to that there was these kinda Irish pubs where you could meet, you could get a job, you could get accommodation, you met a social scene, you had friends immediately, you had someone who knew someone, you'd be from Killala, oh I'm from Crossmolina, I'm from Ballina, whatever, an everyone knew everybody, you were never lost, if you walked into The Roscoe or The Regent on a Sunday lunchtime you were with people, you'd always find whatever you want, you'd get a job no problem that time and that was the kind of scene that people lived in up to 1970 then the Irish Centre took over and you left kinda the Irish music playing in pubs and that, although we started playing the Irish Centre, but that kinda scene was kinda left and you moved into the Irish Centre then where you had big bands coming over from Ireland and a dancehall and weddings were held up there. [Michael, b. 1947, Leeds]

One Donegal man, Lawrence, recalls that these pubs were also collection points and drop off points for labouring men; wagons picked up men in the morning around Sheepscar Corner, at the Sheepscar library and outside the many Irish pubs in this area, depending on which firm they were working for.[74]

A typical Sunday for many Irish emigrants in the city in the 1950s, 1960s and early 1970s was an afternoon in Potternewton Park, Roundhay Park or at Halton Moor. Those in the Sheepscar and Chapeltown areas would then leave Roundhay Park around 5.30pm and get a bus to the Holy Rosary for 6.30pm mass. From here it was home to wash and eat before continuing to the pub; pubs in England were open from 12pm until 2pm and from 7pm until 10.30pm on Sundays. Then onwards to either The Shamrock or St Francis's dancehalls:

So I used to play football up at Halton Moor you see Gaelic football on a Sunday and we used to play Huddersfield and there used to be hard games between Huddersfield and Leeds 'cause there was an awful lot of needle like ya know. And none of the Huddersfield lads liked you taking a girl, a Leeds lad taking a girl from Huddersfield. Oh Jesus you was, oh they'd, they'd kill ya like ya know so I din't know how I'd go on with this craic ... I asked her in anyways, she was in at Halton Moor this Sunday like ya know and I said then we'd been up there all day from two o'clock ... and then we went to Corpus Christi to the mass like you know to the evening mass up there like beside the Halton Moors ... so I says do you want to come back to the aunt's house you know like and we'll go on to we'll wash then and have you know a clean up and then we'll go the dance. [Martin, b. 1940, Co. Mayo]

The social fabric of the Leeds Irish community has changed dramatically over the last fifty years; Michael recalls that the combination of community spread and the introduction of drink driving laws in the 1970s forever changed the city's Irish community:

What took more from the pubs was the fact that as people prospered and moved on in life or whatever, they moved further out and as the breathalyser laws got stricter and stricter an' I mean the old crowd I mean from my era and beyond that, older than me, I mean they had no compunction about driving a car and drinking, it was the thing that everyone was used to doing it in the sixties and there was no breathalyser of course in the early 1970s. So everyone just drink and drove, you did it and that was the way it was ... well that got really keen and people really took it to heart eventually and I think then that stopped the pubs. I mean what they used to do on a Saturday night an' that, go from The Roscoe to The Vic, they'd bring cars I mean they weren't far apart but they'd drive from Harehills down an' people were gettin' cars and gettin' money, drive from there to The Vic, drive down to The Regent, maybe drive up to a Donegal pub, the one up the road, an' maybe drive up to the Irish Centre. Or everyone had a finishing up place, whether it be The Regent, whether it be The Harp, or The Roscoe, or wherever. That stopped then and what you had was people moving out with the breathalyser and people going to the local English pub, so you had them going to local English clubs as well: Labour clubs and Conservative clubs. [Michael, b. 1947, Leeds]

As the Irish community prospered many began to move out of the inner-city areas and into improved residential areas. Generally speaking since the 1970s the Irish have moved out of the Harehills and Chapeltown areas, being replaced by other more recent immigrant groups, particularly Afro-Caribbean and Asian groups. Of course there were those who remained behind; in 1981 Harehills remained the ward with the greatest concentration of Irish, followed by the adjoining wards of Chapel Allerton and Burmantofts. Today the multiracial and multicultural areas of Harehills and Chapeltown are designated Urban Priority Areas and are associated with poor housing, underemployment, drugs, prostitution, crime and race riots. These are problems that are mirrored in other British inner-city areas and council estates.

Notes

1 See: Dr Peter Bell, 'Leeds: The Evolution of a Multi-Cultural Society', *The British Council of Churches, Sixteenth Assembly: 80th Meeting of the Council*, Spring 1982; and Burt and Grady, *The Illustrated History of Leeds*, p. 229.

2 C. J. Morgan, 'Demographic Change', in Fraser (ed.), *A History of Modern Leeds*.

3 In 1827, the Select Committee on Emigration noted that in any major construction project of roads, canals or drains one 'should not feel in the least surprised to find, that of a hundred men employed in it, ninety were Irish'. *Second Report of the Select Committee on Emigration from the United Kingdom*, 1826–27, p. 155.

4 This information on the 'Paddy Line' was gleaned from material gathered for an exhibition entitled 'An Introduction to the Irish in Leeds: An Exhibition of the Irish in Leeds since the 1830s with a Pictorial Display, Parish Registers, Official Documents etc.', which was organised by Leeds City Libraries and Irish in Britain Representation Group and put on display in the Leeds City Library in 1986.

5 Danny and Helen Kennally, 'From Roscrea to Leeds: An Emigrant Community', in *Tipperary Historical Journal*, No. 5, 1992, p. 123.

6 Quoted in Burt and Grady, *The Illustrated History of Leeds*, pp. 155–6, from the *River Pollution Commission 1867*, evidence of Alderman Carter, p. 223.

7 *Report by the Statistical Committee of Town Council*, 1839, in J. F. C. Harrison, *Early Victorian Britain, 1832–51*, 1988, p. 65.

8 *Report by the Statistical Committee of Town Council*, 1839, in Harrison, *Early Victorian Britain, 1832–51*, p. 65.

9 Dillon, 'The Irish in Leeds, 1851–61', p. 7.

10 *Report by the Statistical Committee of Town Council*, 1839, p. 402.

11 *Report by the Statistical Committee of Town Council*, 1839, pp. 401–6.

12 Frederick Engels, *The Condition of the Working Class in England: From Personal Observation and Authentic Sources*, London: Panther, 1976. (no page number)

13 Dillon, 'The Irish in Leeds, 1851–61', pp. 2–3.

14 W. White, *Directory and Gazetteer of Leeds, Bradford, Halifax, and the whole of the Clothing District of Yorkshire*, 1853 (reprinted, Plymouth, 1969), p. 16 from Dillon, 'The Irish in Leeds, 1851–61', p. 2.

15 Alan O'Day (ed.), *A Survey of the Irish in England (1872)*, 1990, p. 66 and p. xxii.

16 Lambert, *Irish Women in Lancashire, 1922–1960*, p. 1.

17 R. Baker, *Report on the State and the Condition of the Town of Leeds*, Parliamentary Papers, XXIX, Sanitary Enquiry, 1842, p.15.

18 Following influenza and typhoid epidemics in 1837 and 1838, Edwin Chadwick was appointed by the government to carry out an enquiry into sanitation; his *Report on the Sanitary Condition of the Labouring Population of Great Britain*, was published in 1842, see David Newsome, *The Victorian World Picture*, 1997, p. 83.

19 J. H. Treble, 'O'Connor, O'Connell and the Attitudes of Irish Immigrants towards Chartism in the North of England', in J. Butt and I. F. Clarke (eds), *The Victorians and Social Protest: A Symposium*, 1973, p. 34.

20 Frank Neal, 'The Famine Irish in England and Wales', in Patrick O'Sullivan (ed.), *The Irish Worldwide. Volume 6: The Meaning of the Famine*, p. 71.

21 Rob Goodbody, *Transactions of the Society of Friends During the Famine in Ireland in 1846 and 1847*, Appendix XV, 1996, p. 380.

22 Christine Kinealy, 'Potatoes, providence and philanthropy', in Patrick O'Sullivan (ed.), *The Irish Worldwide. Volume 6: The Meaning of the Famine*, pp. 155–7.

23 Rev. Edward Jackson, *A Pastor's Recollections*, no. 5, 1890, p.10.

24 Burt and Grady, *The Illustrated History of Leeds*, p. 129.

25 Jackson, *A Pastor's Recollections*, p.11.

26 A. Reach, *Morning Chronicle*, Dec. 1849. In 1849 John Douglas Cook, editor of the *Morning Chronicle*, instigated an investigation into the condition of the labouring classes in England and Wales. Cook recruited a team, which included Angus Reach, whose task it was to investigate the Manufacturing Districts. Reach toured the most important industrial towns (including Leeds, Bradford, Halifax and Sheffield) visiting the homes of the working class. The publication of Reach's writings in the *Morning Chronicle* raised his profile and he gained a reputation as one of Britain's leading journalists.

27 See for example Robert Baker's *Report on the Condition of the Residences of the Labouring Classes in the Town of Leeds* in 1842; and Frederick Engels' *The Condition of the Working Class in England: From Personal Observation and Authentic Sources*, 1976, in which he speaks of the impoverished conditions of the Irish in Leeds in the mid-nineteenth century.

28 Harrison, *Early Victorian Britain, 1832–51*, p. 27.

29 Dillon, 'The Irish in Leeds, 1851–61', p. 15.

30 Roger Swift, 'The Irish in Britain', in Patrick O'Sullivan (ed.), *The Irish Worldwide. Volume 2: The Irish in the New Communities*, p. 65.

31 Dillon, 'The Irish in Leeds, 1851–61', pp. 1–29; Frances Finnegan, *Poverty and Prejudice: A Study of Irish Immigrants in York, 1840–75*, 1982, pp. 132–54; and Clem Richardson, 'The Irish in Victorian Bradford', *The Bradford Antiquary*, 9, 1976, pp. 294–316.

32 Dillon, 'The Irish in Leeds, 1851–61', p. 14.

33 Burt and Grady, *The Illustrated History of Leeds*, p. 170.

34 Burt and Grady, *The Illustrated History of Leeds*, p. 170.

35 J. Mayhall (ed.), *The Annals of Yorkshire: From the earliest period to the present time*, vol. II, 1878, pp. 194–201 in Burt and Grady, *The Illustrated History of Leeds*, p. 156.

36 Patrick O'Farrell, *England and Ireland Since 1800*, 1975, p. 77.

37 Fitch's Report, *Parliamentary Papers*, liv, 357, 1870, p. 89 in Geoffrey Best, *Mid-Victorian Britain, 1851–75*, 1985, pp. 151–2.

38 Dillon, 'The Irish in Leeds, 1851–61', p. 7. The overseer's remark is taken from the *Report from the Select Committee on Irremovable Poor*, P.P., Vol. xvii, 1860, p. 135.

39 From Mayhall (ed.), *The Annals of Yorkshire*, vol. III, pp. 155–7, 159 in Burt and Grady, *The Illustrated History of Leeds*, p. 171.

40 *Leeds Mercury*, 11 May 1895.

41 Mary Patterson, *The Ham Shank*, 1993, p. 3.

42 The Thoresby Society, 'A Brief History of Leeds'. http://www.lapta.co.uk/thoresby/history.htm. Accessed 6 July 2002. Murray Freedman, 'The Leeds Jewish Community: A Sketch of its History and Development' in Lynne Stevenson Tate (ed.), *Aspects of Leeds 1: Discovering Local History*, 1998, p. 171.

43 Freedman, 'The Leeds Jewish Community', p. 170.

44 Bell, 'Leeds: The Evolution of a Multi-Cultural Society', p. 5.

45 King, Shuttleworth and Strachan, 'The Irish in Coventry', p. 75.

46 Pauline E. Freeman, 'Erin's Exiles – The Irish in Leeds', in Robert E. Finnegan and George T. Bradley (eds), *Catholicism in Leeds: A Community of Faith, 1794–1994*, 1994, p. 83.

47 Freeman, 'Erin's Exiles – The Irish in Leeds', p. 75.

48 Treble, 'O'Connor, O'Connell and the Attitudes of Irish Immigrants towards Chartism in the North of England', p. 46.

49 Treble, 'O'Connor, O'Connell and the Attitudes of Irish Immigrants towards Chartism in the North of England', p. 48.

50 http://www.celebrateleeds07.com/downloads/Edpack_victorian.pdf. Accessed 13 March 2007.

51 Thornton, *Leeds: The Story of a City*, p.159.

52 Danny and Helen Kennally, 'From Roscrea to Leeds', p. 130, from *Yorkshire Post*, 5 May, 1937 from an article entitled 'The Bank: Memories of Exciting Times'.

53 Mary J. Hickman, *The Irish Community in Britain: Myth or Reality?*, 1996, p. 7.

54 G. Marshall (ed.), *The Concise Oxford Dictionary of Sociology*, 1994, p. 73.

55 Paul Thompson, *The Voice of the Past: Oral History*, 1978, p. 156.

56 Patterson, *The Ham Shank*, p. 3.

57 Patterson, *The Ham Shank*, p. 10.

58 Danny and Helen Kennally, 'From Roscrea to Leeds', p. 131.

59 See, for example, Chadwick's *Report on the Sanitary Conditions of the Labouring Population of Great Britain* published in 1842 and the first and second *Report of the Commissioners for Enquiring into the State of Large Towns and Populous Districts* published in 1844 and 1845 respectively.

60 Thornton, *Leeds: The Story of a City*, pp. 158–9.

61 Enda Delaney, 'Almost a Class of Helots in an Alien Land: The British State and Irish Emigration, 1921–45', in MacRaild (ed.), *The Great Famine and Beyond*, p. 241.

62 Burt and Grady, *The Illustrated History of Leeds*, p. 207.

63 Mayo is located in the province of Connacht on the west coast of Ireland. The name Mayo derives from the Gaelic *Maigh Eo* meaning 'Plain of the Yew Trees'. It is the third largest county in Ireland (after counties Cork and Galway) with an area of 5,398 sq. km. (2,084 sq. miles) and a population of 117,446 according to the 2004 census. Castlebar is the county town and also the largest town with a population of just 10,287 (2002); Ballina is the second largest town with a population of 9,478 (2002). Traditionally Mayo has been one of the least developed counties in Ireland and it has paid a heavy price for underdevelopment in terms of losing entire communities to emigration.

64 Quoted in Kevin O'Connor, *The Irish in Britain*, 1972, pp. 72–3.

65 Derek Naylor, 'A History Written in Innocent Blood', *Yorkshire Evening Post*, 26 Sept. 1973.

66 Thornton, *Leeds: The Story of a City*, p. 227.

67 Department of Geography and Geology. http://www.brixworth.demon.co.uk/leeds/leeds3.htm. Accessed 13 May 2003.

68 Delaney, *Demography, State and Society*, p. 162.

69 *Yorkshire Evening Post*, 15 June 1967.

70 Bell, 'Leeds: The Evolution of a Multi-Cultural Society', p. 7.

71 Freedman, 'The Leeds Jewish Community', p. 170.

72 Michael Fean, 'Down Memory Lane: Forty Years Ago', in *'Twenty Years a-Growing': Leeds Branch Comhaltas Ceoltóirí Éireann, 1969–1989*, 1989, (no page number).

73 Pearse Hutchinson, 'Leeds or Amsterdam (for Liam Ó Brádaigh)', in D. Kiberd and G. Fitzmaurice (eds), *Crann Faoi Bláth* (*The Flowering Tree*), Dublin: Wolfhound Press, 1991. Pearse Hutchinson was born in Glasgow in 1927 of Irish parents, but reared in Dublin from 1932. The poem, originally penned in Irish, is translated by the author.

74 Lawrence, *b.* 1950, Co. Donegal.

2. Explaining Emigration

And people went from every house, there wasn't any house left that people hadn't gone away from, and it is a shame. When I was driving around and you seen houses that was lovely when you were going to school that were just derelict there, everyone had just gone away and left them. It was such a shame.
[Gráinne, b. 1945, Co. Mayo]

Introduction

The purpose of this chapter is manifold. The primary aim is to investigate the reasons why Irish emigrants left the Republic of Ireland for Britain between 1931 and 1981. Oral historian Alistair Thomson has noted that 'though economic pressures often influence migration decisions, personal testimony reveals the complex weave of factors and influences which contribute to migration'.[1] Thus if the respondent did not offer the information unprompted, they were asked to explain the circumstances of their emigration: how and why they emigrated from Ireland, and how they felt about the move at that time. This chapter also investigates the reasons why Irish emigrants chose Leeds as their direct or indirect destination and highlights some of the problems of settling in the city.

The Extent of Emigration from Ireland

The eminent historian Roy Foster remarked that 'emigration is the great fact of Irish social history from the nineteenth century'.[2] However, it may be argued that migration (that is both emigration and immigration) has been the greatest fact of Irish social history; in fact, prior to the eighteenth century Ireland gained more people than it lost. In recent centuries, however, emigration from Ireland has overshadowed immigration into the country.

Eighteenth-century Irish emigrants made colonial North America their destination. These were predominantly, but by no means exclusively, relatively affluent Presbyterians from the province of Ulster. Their nineteenth-century descendants applied the term 'Scotch-Irish' to their emigrant forefathers to differentiate and distance themselves from those subsequent impoverished Irish Catholic migrants who fled from Ireland from the 1820s.[3] Although estimates vary, it is thought that during the period 1700–76 between 250,000 and 400,000 emigrated from Ireland, which had a mid-century population of around 2.4 million. By the late eighteenth century seasonal migration to Newfoundland and Britain was also an established aspect of Irish life and an integral part of the Irish agricultural economy.[4] Between 1783 and 1815, following the American Revolution, a further 100,000 departed Ireland for the newly independent United States.[5]

It has been noted that Irish emigration over the last two centuries falls into three main temporal waves.[6] The 'first wave' occurred between 1815 and 1920 with Britain and, to an even greater extent, North America the main destinations. The Napoleonic Wars (1803–15) between England and France ensured high war-time prices and brought relative prosperity to Irish agriculture; they were followed by a sharp economic depression and an increased outflow of emigrants. Although the Famine is often viewed as *the* watershed in Irish emigration history, which prompted a mass exodus, by the 1830s large-scale emigration was endemic to all parts of Ireland to an extent unknown anywhere else in Europe: almost 1 million people had left Ireland for North America between 1815 and 1845.[7] British towns and cities, which were prospering from the Industrial Revolution, were also increasingly the destination for Irish emigrants. However, the Famine certainly swelled the numbers of emigrants from Ireland (see Table 2.1) and a combination of death and emigration caused the Irish population to fall from 8.2 million in 1841 to 5.8 million in 1861. North America bore the bulk of the fleeing emigrants: between 1841 and 1860 some 1.7 million Irish had arrived at American seaports; by the time the Irish Free State was established in 1922 a further 2.4 million had joined them.[8]

2. Explaining Emigration

And people went from every house, there wasn't any house left that people hadn't gone away from, and it is a shame. When I was driving around and you seen houses that was lovely when you were going to school that were just derelict there, everyone had just gone away and left them. It was such a shame.
[Gráinne, b. 1945, Co. Mayo]

Introduction

The purpose of this chapter is manifold. The primary aim is to investigate the reasons why Irish emigrants left the Republic of Ireland for Britain between 1931 and 1981. Oral historian Alistair Thomson has noted that 'though economic pressures often influence migration decisions, personal testimony reveals the complex weave of factors and influences which contribute to migration'.[1] Thus if the respondent did not offer the information unprompted, they were asked to explain the circumstances of their emigration: how and why they emigrated from Ireland, and how they felt about the move at that time. This chapter also investigates the reasons why Irish emigrants chose Leeds as their direct or indirect destination and highlights some of the problems of settling in the city.

The Extent of Emigration from Ireland

The eminent historian Roy Foster remarked that 'emigration is the great fact of Irish social history from the nineteenth century'.[2] However, it may be argued that migration (that is both emigration and immigration) has been the greatest fact of Irish social history; in fact, prior to the eighteenth century Ireland gained more people than it lost. In recent centuries, however, emigration from Ireland has overshadowed immigration into the country.

Eighteenth-century Irish emigrants made colonial North America their destination. These were predominantly, but by no means exclusively, relatively affluent Presbyterians from the province of Ulster. Their nineteenth-century descendants applied the term 'Scotch-Irish' to their emigrant forefathers to differentiate and distance themselves from those subsequent impoverished Irish Catholic migrants who fled from Ireland from the 1820s.[3] Although estimates vary, it is thought that during the period 1700–76 between 250,000 and 400,000 emigrated from Ireland, which had a mid-century population of around 2.4 million. By the late eighteenth century seasonal migration to Newfoundland and Britain was also an established aspect of Irish life and an integral part of the Irish agricultural economy.[4] Between 1783 and 1815, following the American Revolution, a further 100,000 departed Ireland for the newly independent United States.[5]

It has been noted that Irish emigration over the last two centuries falls into three main temporal waves.[6] The 'first wave' occurred between 1815 and 1920 with Britain and, to an even greater extent, North America the main destinations. The Napoleonic Wars (1803–15) between England and France ensured high war-time prices and brought relative prosperity to Irish agriculture; they were followed by a sharp economic depression and an increased outflow of emigrants. Although the Famine is often viewed as *the* watershed in Irish emigration history, which prompted a mass exodus, by the 1830s large-scale emigration was endemic to all parts of Ireland to an extent unknown anywhere else in Europe: almost 1 million people had left Ireland for North America between 1815 and 1845.[7] British towns and cities, which were prospering from the Industrial Revolution, were also increasingly the destination for Irish emigrants. However, the Famine certainly swelled the numbers of emigrants from Ireland (see Table 2.1) and a combination of death and emigration caused the Irish population to fall from 8.2 million in 1841 to 5.8 million in 1861. North America bore the bulk of the fleeing emigrants: between 1841 and 1860 some 1.7 million Irish had arrived at American seaports; by the time the Irish Free State was established in 1922 a further 2.4 million had joined them.[8]

Table 2.1: Number of Overseas Emigrants from Ireland (32 Counties): 1825–1860

Years	Total Number of Overseas Emigrants
1825–30	99,968
1831–35	205,299
1836–40	190,182
1841–45	239,751
1846–50	939,609
1851–55	901,206
1856–60	315,059

Source: *Reports of the Commission on Emigration and Other Population Problems, 1948–54*

In total it has been estimated that between 1801 and 1921 almost 8 million people departed Irish shores for new lives in Australia, Britain, Canada, New Zealand and the United States.[9] The result of this mass exodus was that by the early 1920s 43 per cent of Irish-born males and females were living outside of Ireland:

1,037,234	in the United States;
367,747	in England and Wales;
159,020	in Scotland;
105,033	in Australia;
93,301	in Canada;
34,419	in New Zealand;
12,289	in South Africa;
8,414	in India.[10]

This figure of 43 per cent is all the more remarkable when compared to that of other European countries. Comparable figures from other countries with traditions of emigration such as Norway, Scotland and Sweden are 14.8 per cent, 14.1 per cent and 11.2 per cent respectively for 1921; other European countries averaged 4 per cent of their population residing outside of the country of their birth.[11]

From the 1930s Britain became the destination of choice for a 'second wave' of Irish emigrants. The Great Depression of the 1930s and the introduction of immigration quotas greatly reduced the numbers of Irish migrating to the United States; furthermore, disruptions to transatlantic travel during the war curbed emigration to the US and elsewhere.[12] Increased labour demands throughout the war years and in the post-war re-building of Britain resulted in a surge of emigration from Ireland; by 1951 there were over half a million people born in the Republic of Ireland residing in Britain, peaking at over 725,000 in 1961 (see Table 2.2). Ireland's geographical position between the two great labour markets of the world, Britain and North America, and the fact that for many generations usually both, but at least one, of these markets have allowed Irish people unrestricted access has facilitated Irish emigration.[13] The third wave (known also as the 'new wave') refers to renewed emigration in the 1980s and falls outside the time period under consideration in this book.

Table 2.2: Irish-born Residents in Britain: 1931–81

Census	Born in Irish Republic	Born in Northern Ireland	Total
1931	367,424	137,961	505,385
1941	No Census	No Census	No Census
1951	537,709	178,319	716,028
1961	726,121	224,857	950,978
1971	709,235	248,595	957,830
1981	607,428	242,969	850,397

Source: *Census of Population of England and Wales: 1931-1981*

Commission on Emigration and Other Population Problems, 1948–54

It is useful at this point to mention the most important governmental document regarding twentieth-century Irish emigration. In 1947 a concerned Pope Pius XII raised the issue of mass emigration from Ireland. This overt concern would have caused much embarrassment to the devout de Valera and his government.[14] However, de Valera did not get the immediate chance to remedy the situation; the Commission on Emigration and Other Population Problems was established in 1948, not by Fianna Fáil but by the recently formed inter-party government of Fine Gael, Labour and other minority parties headed by John A. Costello. It proved to be the Irish government's most energetic and assertive attempt to explore the root causes of emigration. The inclusion of 'Other Population Problems' in the title implies that the government viewed emigration as an undesirable trend. The economist Dr James Beddy chaired the Commission of twenty-four members that included statisticians, economists, medical doctors, union officials, a number of government officials, writers, social critics, clergymen and a sociologist. Notably, despite the fact that for the period 1926–51 female emigrants outnumbered their male counterparts, the panel contained just two women. Furthermore, it was pointed out in the *Irish Press* that of those who made up the panel the majority had 'little direct knowledge of the problem to be solved'.[15]

The Commission convened on over a hundred occasions. Impending emigrants were interviewed and the social conditions throughout various parts of the country were surveyed. The Commission did not bring about an end to Irish emigration, in fact in terms of numbers the worst was yet to come, but 'it did contribute to a more realistic understanding of its causes'.[16]

Who Left Ireland?

The Geographical Origin of Irish Emigrants

Throughout the period under consideration the western provinces of Munster and Connacht supplied the bulk of emigrants. From the reports published by the Commission on Emigration the six counties with the highest volume of net emigration for the period 1926–36 were (in order) Cork, Mayo, Kerry, Donegal, Galway and Tipperary, these being in total responsible for 62 per cent of net emigration.[17] For the period 1936–46 the order changed slightly: Cork, Mayo, Galway, Kerry, Donegal and Limerick, accounting for 52 per cent of net emigration.[18] Finally, for the period 1946–51 they were again similar: Cork, Galway, Kerry, Mayo, Donegal and Limerick, constituting 55 per cent of net emigration.[19] Although all Irish counties were affected by emigration, it can be seen that the western seaboard counties of Cork, Mayo, Donegal, Kerry and Galway are over-represented for the period 1926–51. Whilst not all migration was rural in origin the majority of emigrants were from a farming background. The Commission on Emigration noted that those counties with densely populated, poor quality land and relatively little urbanisation, particularly those on the western seaboard of Ireland, were most susceptible to emigration:

Most of the counties which have had high rates of emigration have also some or all of the following characteristics – heavy density of rural population, low valuation of agricultural land per head, high percentage of population living in rural areas and high percentage of agricultural areas in small holdings.[20]

However, these statistics are in absolute and not relative terms. The counties that had the highest average annual rate of net emigration per 1,000 of the population from the end of the Second World War were for the intercensal period 1946–51 (in order) Leitrim, Kerry, Longford, Roscommon and Clare. In the 1950s, for the period 1951–56 they were Leitrim, Donegal, Monaghan, Mayo and Wicklow; for the period 1956–61 they were Monaghan, Leitrim, Cavan, Longford and Mayo. In the 1960s for the period 1961–66 they were Leitrim, Mayo, Longford, Donegal and Cavan, and finally for the period 1966–71 they were Leitrim, Mayo, Offaly, Longford and Roscommon.[21] As can be seen Leitrim, Mayo, Longford and Cavan are over-represented in relative terms and again western counties are over-represented.

The majority of the respondents in this oral history sample conform to the pattern of emigrants originating from the western seaboard counties of Ireland (see Appendices); of the sample of thirty-three respondents who provided life testimonies, twenty-one hailed western seaboard counties (64 per cent), five from Dublin City (15 per cent) and seven from elsewhere in Ireland (21 per cent). John A. Jackson noted in his seminal study of the Irish in Britain that 'the background from which the Irish immigrant to Great Britain has come has, in the main, been a rural one. This background has done little to prepare the immigrant for urban life in Britain but it is to this life that he has been constantly attracted'.[22] Furthermore, twenty-five respondents came from rural areas (76 per cent), three came from county towns (9 per cent) and five came from the city of Dublin (15 per cent). The relatively high number of five emigrants from Dublin does not, however, correspond with the general trend of Irish emigration. The pattern of 'second-wave' female emigration is generally seen to be the same as that of their male counterparts with the exception that male emigration from urban areas, particularly Dublin, was higher whilst that of rural areas was lower.[23]

The years in which the respondents departed Ireland range from 1933 to 1978, with the vast majority (82 per cent) emigrating before 1963. Table 2.3 highlights the decennial breakdown of respondents' first year of departure.

Table 2.3: Decennial Breakdown of Respondents First Year of Departure

Decennial Period	No. of Respondents
1931–40	7
1941–50	5
1951–60	9
1961–70	11
1971–80	1

Source: Interviews with respondents

Gender Distribution of Irish Emigrants

Between 1901 and 1971, with the exception of two intercensal periods (1911–26 and 1936–46), female emigrants outnumbered their male counterparts (see Table 2.4); these two periods correspond with major British overseas conflicts during which time many Irishmen were recruited into the British Army.[24] Additionally, female emigration was subject to restrictions during the war years; for example, Irish females under twenty-two years of age were only permitted to emigrate if they were going to train as teachers, nurses or midwives and only women over the age of twenty-two were allowed to take up work in the factories of Britain.[25] Nonetheless, for the majority of the period female emigrants outnumbered their male counterparts; this was despite suggestions by the church that steps should be taken by the government to curb female emigration.[26] Of the thirty-three emigrant life stories recorded here, eighteen or 45.5 per cent were female.

Table 2.4: Annual Net Emigration from Ireland: 1926–1981

Period	Annual net emigration		
	Males	Females	Total
1926–36	- 7,255	- 9,420	- 16,675
1936–46	- 11,258	- 7,454	- 18,712
1947–51	- 10,309	- 14,075	- 24,384
1951–56	- 21,657	- 17,696	- 39,353
1956–61	- 21,914	- 20,486	- 42,400
1961–66	- 7,523	- 8,598	-16,121
1966–71	- 4,950	- 5,831	-10,781
1971–79	+ 7,659	+ 5,958	+ 13,617
1979–81	- 1,606	- 6,345	- 2,523

Source: P. J. Drudy, 'Migration between Ireland and Britain since Independence', in P. J. Drudy (ed.), *Irish Studies 5: Ireland and Britain Since 1922*, 1986, p. 109

Age Distribution of Irish Emigrants

Family emigration (that of adults and children moving together) was predominant during the Famine years; this pattern drastically declined from the 1890s when young adults between the ages of fifteen and twenty-four began to constitute the bulk of the emigrants and continued throughout the period covered here.[27] Between 1924 and 1939, 54 per cent of all Irish emigrants were in the fifteen and twenty-four age group and a further 16 per cent were in the twenty-five to twenty-nine category.[28] From 1939 to 1952, Irish emigrants who intended to travel to Britain were obliged to obtain travel and employment permits or travel identity cards. In the 1940s there was a noticeable increase in the emigration of older males to Britain in contrast to the continued predominance of younger females; of those who received travel permits between 1943 and 1951, 46 per cent of males and 69 per cent of females were under twenty-five years of age.[29] As a result of war-time restrictions family emigration all but disappeared but reappeared again in the 1950s, whereas the emigration of older Irish males declined.[30] This oral history sample generally corresponds to the trends outlined above. Of the sample of thirty-three, eight persons left Ireland under the age of fifteen as part of a family. Excluding those who left as part of a family, 92 per cent of the female respondents emigrated from Ireland between the ages of fifteen and twenty-four. Similarly 92 per cent of the male respondents first left Ireland aged between fifteen and twenty-four.

Explanations for Emigration

During the fifty-year period under consideration around one million people emigrated from the Republic of Ireland, the vast majority relocating to Britain; it is estimated that since 1900 two out of every three Irish emigrants made Britain their destination.[31] Why did so many people leave Ireland? And why did they migrate to certain regions?

The 1950s' *Reports of the Commission on Emigration* identified economic reasons as the root cause of emigration, adding, however, that in the majority of cases the decision to leave Ireland could not be regarded as belonging to any one motive but to the interplay of several motives.[32] The authors further qualified this statement by ascribing social, political, cultural and psychological causes, as well as economic, to emigration. The authors of the *Reports* recognised that the 'push-pull' model that was used to explain migration was unsatisfactory in that 'both forces operate together even in the case of an individual, and taking the country as a whole it is extremely difficult to decide which of them has been the more potent'.[33] However, they concluded that at some periods the 'push' factor was the predominant force influencing

Serial No. A15265

CÁRTA AITHEANTAIS TAISTIL.
TRAVEL IDENTITY CARD.

Le h-ágaidh Taistil idir Éire agus
Bhreatáin Mhór amháin.

*For Travel between Ireland and Great
Britain only.*

Bailí ar feadh cúig bliana ó dáta eisiúna.

Valid for five years from date of issue.

Serial Number A15265

Sloinne / *Surname* — KEENAN

Ainmneacha / *Christian Name* — Mary Theresa

Sloinne a hAthar / *Maiden Name* —

Seoladh / *Address* — 91 Ferguson Road Drumcondra, Dublin

Gairm / *Profession* — Civil Servant

Dáta Breithe / *Date of Birth* — 15/10/1919

Áit Bhreithe / *Place of Birth* — Offaly

Siniú an tSealbhóra / *Signature of Holder* — Mary T. Keenan

Dáta Eisiúna / *Date of Issue* — 21st April 1948

GARDA SÍOCHÁNA PASSPORT OFFICE 21 APR 1948 DUBLIN CASTLE Metropolitan Division

Travel Identity Card. Courtesy of Ultan Cowley

K 36817

CÁRTA CEAD TAISTIL.
TRAVEL PERMIT CARD.

Chun Taistil idir Éire agus an Ríocht
Aontaithe amháin.
For Travel between Ireland and the United
Kingdom only.
See Page

Éire

Ainm an tSealbhóra
Name of Holder

Mary Theresa KEENAN

FOLÁIREAMH.

1. Ní thugann an Cárta Cead Taistil seo ceart don tsealbhóir dul isteach sa mBreatain Mhór ná fíltear mura mbíd leigníolacha air via Bhreatanach chun data isteach sa mBreatain Mhóir nó mura imeacta Bhreatanach bailí chun fillte ar an mBreatain Mhóir gun cead imeachta.

2. Ní thugann an Cárta Cead Taistil seo ceart don tsealbhóir an Bhreatain Mhór d'fhágáil mura mbíd fíormhcáithe air cead imeachta Bhreatanach chun imeachta as an mBreatain Mhóir nó via Bhreatanach bailí chun fillte ar Éirinn ón mBreatain Mhóir gun cead imeachta.

3. Ba chóir via Bhreatanach d'iarraidh ar—

An Cread-Oifig Bhreatainach,
30, Cearnóg Mhuirbhthean,
Baile Átha Cliath.

Ba chóir cead imeachta Bhreatanach d'arraidh ar cheann de na hoifigí seo leanas:—

Londra (London):
THE PASSPORT AND PERMIT OFFICE,
1, Queen Anne's Gate Buildings,
Dartmouth Street S.W.1.

Learpholl (Liverpool):
THE BRANCH PASSPORT AND PERMIT OFFICE,
26, Dale Street.

Glascú (Glasgow):
THE PERMIT OFFICE,
10, Bothwell Street, C.2.

4. Ní threastóir via ar an gCárta Cead Taistil seo chun dul isteach i dTuaisceart Éireann muna mbíd an tsealbhóir ag taisteal ón mBreatain Mhóir

WARNING.

1. This Travel Permit Card does not entitle the holder to enter Great Britain from Ireland unless it bears endorsed thereon either a British visa for entry into Great Britain visa for entry into Great Britain or a British exit permit valid for return to Great Britain without a visa.

2. This Travel Permit Card does not entitle the holder to depart from Great Britain unless it bears endorsed thereon either a British exit permit for departure from Great Britain or a British visa valid for return to Ireland from Great Britain without an exit permit.

3. Application for a British visa should be made to—

THE BRITISH PERMIT OFFICE,
30, Merrion Square,
Dublin.

Application for a British exit permit should be made to any of the following offices:—

4. This Travel Permit Card does not require a visa for entry into Northern Ireland unless the holder is travelling from Great Britain.

K 36817

To an leabhrán so leathtear ar. This booklet contains 20 pages.

SONNRAÍ DEN tSEALBHÓIR.
PARTICULARS OF HOLDER.

Ainm / Name — Mary Theresa Keenan

Uathshloinne / Maiden Name —

Gairm / Occupation — Civil Servant

Seoladh baile / Home Address — 91 Ferguson Road Drumcondra Dublin

Áit bhreithe / Place of Birth — Eden derry Offaly

Dáta breithe / Date of Birth — 15. 10. 1919

Saoránacht / Citizenship — CITIZEN OF IRELAND

Áit agus dáta a thabhartha amach :
Place and date of issue :

DUBLIN 5 JUL 1945 DEPARTMENT OF EXTERNAL AFFAIRS

Caithfear bailíocht an Chárta Cead Taistil seo ar an
The validity of this Travel Permit Card expires on the

5 JUL 1946

muna n-athnuaitear é.
unless renewed.

Travel Permit Card. Courtesy of Ultan Cowley

emigration whilst at others it was the 'pull' factor: 'It was undoubtedly a "push" during and after the Famine and following poor harvests, whereas there was a strong element of "pull" during periods of full employment in Great Britain'.[34]

Undoubtedly, both male and female emigration was fuelled largely by the same general factors: the mass availability of work in Britain and the disparity in wage levels between the two countries. In the 1920s and 1930s 'one out of every two persons born in the twenty-six county state failed to secure permanent employment there';[35] the alternatives were to take the boat or to remain at home and endure 'chronic idleness'. For those who emigrated, wages in Britain were substantially higher than in Ireland during the war and in the immediate post-war years; in fact The Emergency orders restricted wage levels in Ireland.[36] Cormac Ó Gráda, when comparing industry-wide levels in 1938 and 1946, noted that the difference between Irish and British wages increased from 16 per cent to 32 per cent for males, whilst that of females increased from 8 per cent to 31 per cent.[37] The establishment of the modern British Welfare State by the Labour government in the second half of the 1940s also ensured better conditions for the working classes in Britain. Successive Acts of Parliament sought to counter the 'five giant evils of Want, Disease, Squalor, Ignorance and Idleness' with its 'five giants on the road to recovery': social security, a national health service, housing provision, state education and a commitment to full employment.[38] The Irish were even better off on the dole in post-war Britain than at home as unemployment money in Britain was double that of Ireland.[39] In contrast the 1940s and 1950s are remembered as decades of 'turmoil and malaise' in Ireland.[40] The economic conflicts which dominated Anglo-Irish relations throughout the 1930s were finally resolved in 1938 and the following year the long expected world war began. Consequently, it wasn't until 1945 that the Irish government could begin to operate in terms of expansion rather than mere subsistence. Slowly and laboriously, the new State faced the gargantuan task of creating an effective infrastructure (housing, social welfare services, hospitals, health care, electric power, roads, transport and communications), without which economic development could not take place. However, for many these changes were too little, too late and tens of thousands of de Valera's 'comely maidens' and 'athletic youths' swapped the 'frugal comforts' of rural Ireland for the materialistic comforts of urban Britain. The 1950s in Ireland were primarily characterised by 'severe economic difficulties, difficulties which were exacerbated by the political instability of the period',[41] emigration levels soared and the population of the State plummeted to 2.9 million. Essentially for much of the period under consideration Irish emigrants were moving from a static economy to a dynamic economy in Britain.

As previously mentioned the oral history respondents were asked to explain the circumstances of their emigration. The following sections deal with the explanations given by the respondents. Male and female responses are dealt with separately because, as the Commission on Emigration acknowledged, male and female emigration was often influenced by different factors.

Although female emigration, like male, is the result of a variety of causes, the purely economic cause is not always so dominant. For the female emigrant improvement in personal status is of no less importance than higher wages and better conditions of employment abroad.[42]

Female Emigration

For the majority of the female respondents interviewed there were two main reasons cited for needing or wanting to emigrate. There seemed to be a strong desire first to be independent and, second, to better themselves and Britain it appeared provided better opportunities for individual improvement:

When I, you know, got old enough I wanted to do me own thing and I left Ireland, I come over here in 1959. [Nuala, b. 1931, Co. Wexford]

Well I wasn't making anything of my life there and I wanted to get on a bit you see. [Clare, b. 1913, Co. Leitrim]

The majority of the women interviewed had left school in their early teens, and sometimes as young as eleven, to help on the family farm, take up employment locally or to look after an ill or aged family member. Several of the women spoke of dissatisfaction with the education they received and the fact that farm-work often took precedence:

Well between going and coming, we may as well stay at home, because what we learned was nothing, some days our books were never looked at. It was shocking, you know, to bring ya family up like that, we'd be out, if it was a nice day, we'd be out saving turf for the winter and bringing it in, made bring it in as well, you know, and store for the winter inside. [Eithne, b. 1911, Co. Mayo]

Almost all of the women had worked at home on the farm or in near-by towns as domestics or childminders for a few years before deciding to migrate to Britain. In many cases it was the experience of working in these menial jobs that led to the decision to leave Ireland. Eithne left school at eleven and worked on the family farm for a decade before leaving for Leeds:

Well we done the farm, we were on the farm; there were nothing else to do until I come here. [Eithne, b. 1911, Co. Mayo]

Eileen, at thirteen years of age, was forced by economic necessity to leave school early and take up a position locally as a childminder:

She was offering a pound a month and you were a skivvy, you weren't looking after children you were doing everything, you were dusting, polishing, cleaning, everything and washing, oh it was horrible ... then I left there 'cause I was just a skivvy and I thought I would be just looking after the children ... and I left there and I went to Killala to a teacher there and her, they were both teachers but they had a big family and the grandmother was looking after the children, they wanted help, well help was just another skivvy [laughs] **so you know I just got tired of it and I wrote to me mother and I said, 'Come down with the sidecar and take me home from this blooming place', I said. I stuck it about six months, I said 'I'm tired and tired of working and being a skivvy for them', and there was seven or eight children in it, you know, it was hard going and I was only a kid meself but they expected you to work there like a slave so I left there and then I went to Ballina to another teacher and his wife.** [Eileen, b. 1918, Co. Mayo]

There was a distinct lack of opportunity available to women in the newly independent Ireland and the fact of the matter was that they were unwilling to spend their lives eking a meagre living from the land. In 1936 there were 19,000 female relatives working on the farms of Connacht, by 1951 this figure had fallen to less than 9,000; whilst the number of female relatives had decreased by more than 50 per cent, only 25 per cent of male relatives departed during the same period.[43] Britain afforded more employment opportunities to women than Ireland; Delia realised that staying at home in Mayo left her with few options:

I think if I'd stayed at home I end up as a waitress or a cleaner or something because, or maybe a shop assistant, serve me time for two years, you know, working for ten shillings a week or something 'cos that's how it was then, they expected you to serve your time as a shop assistant... [but] the idea of doing nursing and having a profession was more important I thought. [Delia, b. 1934, Co. Mayo]

Bridget, also from Mayo, concurs with Delia in that working as a shopkeeper's apprentice offered little attraction or long-term security:

In those days [1930s] you'd have to pay to be an apprentice for three years and afterwards they might let you go; that wasn't for me. [Bridget, b. 1918, Co. Mayo]

Honora's uncle sent her passage to America when she was fifteen; however, Honora's mother refused to let her go to America because she was so young. Instead she was sent to Tuam in Co. Galway to work as a shopkeeper's assistant:

When I was about, I think I was fifteen when I went into Tuam, me uncle Denis, he never got married and he was me Godfather, he sent me passage from America and because in them days you had to do what your parents told ya, and without your parents permission you had to be twenty-one, even to come to England in them days an' you had to have a letter from your parish priest to a parish priest over here, all the lot, all the paraphernalia, because they used to say if girls came to London they were put in the white slave traffic as prostitutes, now whether it was right or not or whether it was just fairy tales I don't know ... me mam wouldn't let me go until I was twenty-one, in the meantime she sent me in to Tuam to serve me time in a shop called John Burke's in Tuam, she said 'the way you'll have something to your back if you do go to America'. And in them days you had to call the boss 'Sir' and you had to be in at night no later than nine o'clock. [Honora, b. 1914, Co. Galway]

Within Article 41 of the 1937 *Constitution of Ireland*, which replaced the 1922 *Constitution of the Irish Free State*, the 'official' role of females was enshrined identifying all women with motherhood and domesticity. However, not all women were willing to accept their assigned roles; they wanted more from their lives and felt that Britain afforded them a better opportunity. Eithne explained her reason for leaving Ireland:

Well there were nothing to do and you know and they wanted you to get married at home and be in poverty again; so it was no use being like that. So I didn't want that; I wanted to travel. So I did. [Eithne, b. 1911, Co. Mayo]

Several of the women expressed dissatisfaction with their lives in Ireland; they wanted what they felt they could not achieve in Ireland: independence and betterment. Agnes's story is typical of those related by many of the female respondents; it's a story which expresses a desire to be autonomous whilst being restrained by familial and social circumstances. Agnes grew up on a ninety-two acre farm in Co. Roscommon in the 1920s and early 1930s; the family's income from agriculture was supplemented by her father's army pension. Growing up she wanted to be a nurse but her mother was 'kind of an invalid all her life' and her father decided that she would stay at home and look after her. Agnes realises that the family was relatively well off but she desired independence:

I really had a good life, a wonderful life, you know, in comparison to some people, but I didn't want it. I wanted to do something for myself. [Agnes, b. 1918, Co. Roscommon]

However, independence was not easily obtained as family commitments and expectations bound her at home. Unbeknownst to her parents, Agnes used to reply to newspaper advertisements recruiting trainees in a variety of positions. Her father discovered one of these letters one day and responded:

'You? Work!' he says 'in there', he said, 'a hairdressers, you wouldn't earn enough money to keep you in nylon stockings'. [Agnes, b. 1918, Co. Roscommon]

So that was ruled out for her. Furthermore, Agnes was secretly meeting a Donegal man, whom she later married in Leeds, but again her parents exercised control in this aspect of her life:

In them days they didn't believe in courtship or anything; they only believed in, you know, matchmaking, making, you know, matches ... I might be wrong, I might have judged them wrong but I always thought they [parents] **wanted me to marry this man you know and he was a lot older than me. He was a cattle jobber. And he used to take these cattle to the station; send them all over, you know, export them and all this. I always thought now this is what they had in their minds. If you think this, I'm not having it!** [Agnes, b. 1918, Co. Roscommon]

One day in 1938, Agnes, aged twenty years, decided that she'd had enough of being told what to do; as was usual Agnes went to collect her father's army pension, she handed in his pension book and used the money to go to England. Although, her sudden unannounced departure was untypical, her motives were similar to many of the other female respondents. Agnes's account of her departure, as with those of other respondents, is neither simple nor straightforward but involves a number of competing elements.

Almost all of the female respondents left Ireland single in their late teens or early twenties; this corresponds with one of the unique features of Irish emigration:

Unlike females in other ethnic groups, Irish females do not leave the country of their birth as part of a family, that is as wives and daughters of the males who have emigrated to find work. Most of them emigrate as economically active young, single females.[44]

For these females the towns and cities of Britain offered almost unlimited employment opportunities for both the skilled and unskilled worker in factories and hospitals, shops and restaurants, on trams and buses, as domestics and cleaners.

There were other reasons too that a woman might emigrate; one such reason was to conceal a pregnancy outside of marriage. Sex and sexuality were taboo subjects in the decades after Independence and contraceptives and abortions were condemned by church and state. Consequently unmarried mothers were often ostracised by family and community and many chose to flee to Britain rather than cause embarrassment to their family:

I was twelve; I didn't know where babies come from. I thought the nurse brought them in the big black bag at the back of the bicycle; I didn't know, I knew nothing about it, we knew nothing ... and if a girl had a baby out of wedlock at home she never came back to the village – 'Oh what would the neighbours say' – they lived for the neighbours in them days, especially in the country.
[Honora, b. 1914, Co. Galway]

Male Emigration

The majority of the male respondents finished their education in their early teens; according to *Investment in Education*, 82 per cent of Irish-born residents in Britain in 1961 had left school at the age of fifteen or under.[45] It appears to have been common practice to keep young males at home from school when the farm-work required extra pairs of hands. Austin finally left school at thirteen but recalls that:

I finished school early 'cause I was the oldest of the family and whenever there was turf to be saved, or turf to be spread, or hay to be made I was kept at home from school to help on the farm, so I didn't get no schooling at all. I got a schooling but not what you'd call a right schooling, ya know.
[Austin, b. 1916, Co. Roscommon]

Although Owen is almost three decades Austin's junior his reminiscences are similar:

I went to school in Straide, but only just the national school, twelve I left … that was alright like you know I was glad to get away from it. They say that your school days is the best days of yer life, they weren't for me. I was glad to got out, I was kept home half the time anyway, like you know, the father'd say, if it was a fine day, 'take this day off now Owen and we'll go to the bog' or 'take this day off and we'll go to the haymaking' and if it was raining then I'd be ran out to school. [Owen, b. 1943, Co. Mayo]

Post-education opportunities were also limited for males; those from moneyed backgrounds could continue to second-level education, some found occasional work locally, whilst others moved to Dublin. However, many spent a period on the farm at home, worked as part-time farmers and seasonal migrants or emigrated permanently to Britain. In contrast in Britain there was a seemingly insatiable demand for labour on construction sites or on the massive civil engineering projects in the decades after the war. The journalist and social commentator John Healy noted of males from rural backgrounds that: 'as soon as he could he left primary school for he was "wanted at home", to mould spuds, to make hay, to save turf. In due time he would go to Lincolnshire to the farmer, often with his father or older brother and the town would not miss him'.[46] Furthermore, traditionally the eldest son inherited the farm so for the others staying on the farm was not a long-term option; Honora explains that the younger of her two brothers had to emigrate:

You see he was the second son, it's only our Michael that could stay on the farm. He had to get a job outside and all us girls had to leave. Only the oldest son could stay on the place. [Honora, b. 1914, Co. Galway]

Agnes too recalls this common practice; she had one sister and two brothers and recalls that:

My brother and sister went to America. In them days there was two was sent away to America and the other two was married. And in them days the arrangement was, you know, was one would have the place and the other one got a fortune. [Agnes, b. 1918, Co. Roscommon]

The paradoxical result was that the younger siblings often felt bitter about having to emigrate whilst the eldest regretted having to stay on the farm, both feeling that they had been given a worse deal.

Economic reasons featured strongly amongst the male respondents for having or desiring to leave Ireland. Additionally, if there was a family or local tradition of emigration the respondent appeared to follow the pattern without reflecting on why they were leaving. John A. Jackson writing in the early 1960s realised the effect that returning emigrants were having on those left behind at home:

An important factor in deciding the girls to go, and this is equally true of the men, is likely to be the contact they have with return emigrants … back for their holidays from English cities and already urbanites, in appearance 'grand' and sophisticated in contrast to those left at home. Life in Britain appeared more attractive and those who returned do little to discourage others from following.[47]

This is certainly true and the influence of the returning emigrant with money to burn, or at least superficially so, was a strong draw on the prospective emigrant. One Mayo man who emigrated in 1960 describes exactly what it was about the returning emigrant that influenced his decision to go:

Well everyone was comin' that time, all me mates was going away like you know, an' I just wanted to see it, to see what it was like. I seen them all comin' home with black fuckin' suits on them and lovely ties, and rakes of money, an' takin' all the women off the young bucks at home – all the lads that had no money – comin' home an' hiring cars out and all this, Jayz sure you'd definitely go or want to go, if you were able like. [Owen, b. 1943, Co. Mayo]

To Owen it appeared that everyone was going to England, particularly those of his own age (late teens and early twenties). For Owen it wasn't so much that the returned emigrant seemed 'grand' or more 'sophisticated' but that they were flashing their earnings, were well dressed and were wooing the local girls away from the local boys when they were home. He further recalls that as the second of nine children reared on a twenty-five acre farm there was little resistance at home to his going:

And there was no such thing as being stopped goin', they'd be glad to get rid of ya [laughs] ... too many mouths around the table. [Owen, b. 1943, Co. Mayo]

A sense of adventure and a desire 'to see what it was like' also drew many young males across the Irish Sea. Jeremiah had a relatively prosperous car-hire business in Monaghan town in the 1950s but decided to leave and join his brother who worked as a watchmaker in Sheffield:

Many a chap had to go because he couldn't get work but I had a little business going ... I fancied to see what the other side of the globe was like. [Jeremiah, b. 1932, Co. Monaghan]

Another, less documented, reason that a young man might emigrate was when it was to avoid a jail term; in many cases the excuse that the offender was soon to be taking the boat was sufficient to escape the long arm of the law:

At that time if a fella was up in court one of the pleas in his defence to let him off and not give him a sentence was 'leave him off your honour he's going to England tomorrow morning' as if like this was a mitigating circumstance, he was goin' to be out of the way, we were going to export our criminals, in inverted commas, off over to England, to the old enemy, so I can remember that like very well and if you go back and you read these stories in the paper at that time you'll find those fairly common. I can think of one like, as I talk to you, I can think of one lad in particular who got into a bit of bother, now by modern day standards it would be harmless fun in our time but maybe at that time it wasn't seen as such harmless fun. I mean there was no malice, there was no personal injury, there might be injury to property a little bit but it was borne out of maybe boredom, frustration, all the things that adolescents have when they grow up if they don't have outlets for them and he ended up in America ... he was a local lad well known to us all ... that would have been very much part and parcel of our environment at that time [1950s]. [Fr. Dominic, b. 1947, Co. Kerry]

Why Did Irish Emigrants Go to Leeds?

As has been highlighted in chapter three, Leeds had a tradition of Irish settlement from the early 1800s: the 1841 census recorded 5,027 Irish-born persons in Leeds Borough; by 1861 this figure had increased to 10,333 persons. Thereafter there was a decline in the number of Irish-born persons in Leeds in both absolute and relative terms, falling to just 3,165 in 1931. As may be seen in Table 2.5 the Irish-born population of the city greatly increased between 1931 and 1961 (by 110 per cent), peaking in 1971 at 7,580 persons.

Table 2.5: Irish-born Population of Leeds (County Borough): 1931–81

Census Year	Irish-born Population	% Change of Irish-born Population	Total Population of Leeds
1931	3,165	n/a	482,809
1941	No Census	No Census	No Census
1951	4,788	+ 51.3	505,219
1961	6,632	+ 38.5	510,676
1971	7,580	+ 14.3	496,009
1981*	7,563	- 0.2	696,714

Source: *Census of Population of England and Wales*: 1921–1981, County Reports

Again, if the respondents did not offer the information unprompted, they were asked to explain why they migrated, either directly or indirectly, to Leeds. It transpired that Britain was not the first choice of destination for some of the older emigrants interviewed; several of the respondents had initially hoped to join elder siblings or relations who had emigrated to the United States (other respondents had parents who spent some time in America and later returned to Ireland). Eithne had hoped to follow her siblings to the US but immigration restrictions prevented her from doing so; a series of quota restrictions were imposed from 1921 and in 1930 measures were introduced which excluded immigrants who lacked finances and/or prospective employment.[48]

There was four older than me, two brothers an' two sisters, an' they went to, me brother, me sisters went to America an' I wanted to go then, ya know but it was closed so I had to, I come here instead … I thought I might get to America, ya know, but then me sisters in America tried to get me out there but I'm glad I didn't now because when I was out in America I didn't like it. I didn't like American ways, they were all bluffing ya know, an' what they had an' what they hadn't an' they hadn't half the things we had. Ya know an' they had it in their mind that we were down an' out here ya know an' we weren't ya know. We had as nice a place as they have had out there. [Eithne, b. 1911, Co. Mayo]

Furthermore, of those who chose to go to England it transpired that Leeds was often not the first destination for many of the respondents; almost two-thirds of those interviewed initially emigrated to places other than Leeds (see Appendix 3: Table A9). So how and why did these emigrants eventually end up in this city?

Many of the older male respondents who left Ireland from the 1930s to 1950s initially went with family members or in local gangs to work in the fields of Britain. The arduous work was seasonal, usually from the end of May until November, and could include anything from haymaking to potato picking, milking cows, mucking out, beet hoeing, dyke mowing and harvesting. Several of the male respondents had worked as farm labourers throughout Britain before eventually settling in Leeds. Austin emigrated to Chester in 1937 and found work as a farm labourer; he stayed on the farm and lived in a shant.[49]

Farm-work, milking cows and mucking out an' all that kind of thing ya know, an' then it was the haytime ya know ... I stayed in a shant and a nice one an' I tell ya what was nice about it, I was lucky. It was a harness room, you see where they used to keep the harness and they kept horses there before my time and it was a harness room and there was a fireplace and a fine bed an' bed clothes, everything an' you got a Sunday dinner as well, they cooked a Sunday dinner for ya, you did your own cooking like up to that but you could have a bath up at the farmhouse ... £2 a week, well it was and it wasn't [good money] for the hours you see ya worked Sunday an' all ya know, it wasn't great, naw! [Austin, b. 1916, Co. Roscommon]

From their early teens Seamus and his brother went 'tattie hoking' (potato digging) to Scotland with their parents but they eventually went their own way; in the mid-1950s they moved south of the boarder to England:

When we [Seamus and his brother] got up to seventeen and eighteen we went our own way, we came to England, we head for, what do you call it, we head for Lincolnshire for the farmers, we used to go to the farmers then ... we used to do eight weeks at the beet, the sugar beet; we'd go then we'd go to this farmer outside Peterborough called Marsh an' we'd mow dykes for him ... he'd pay us so much a chain, it was more or less piece work. An' then we'd be at him for a few weeks and then we'd leave him and we'd go back to this farmer that we hoed the beet at an' we'd, we used do harvest for him, he had horses and carts and he used to have, what do you call it, a machine an' it used to cut wheat and we'd go after an' we'd make stooks o' it, in the field. An' then when we'd finished all the making, maybe sixty or seventy acres he had a horse and cart and there was two of us then, one on the bottom, me brother on the bottom, me on the top and I'd build it and bring it into the farm ... it was a hard auld life too, wasn't it? ... There was six o' us that went to the farmer there, picking spuds, we done the beet ... the six o' us used to cook together an' we had two double beds, three o' us in each bed, yes [laughs] yeah the three o' us in each bed; we had a big hut ... We were on good money, I mean like, the money we were on that time was the only way we could make the money, we were on piece work, whatever we'd earn we'd have to go for it even when we were picking spuds, we'd get so much an acre o' spuds and we'd ... make a good week's wages. [Seamus, b. 1936, Co. Mayo]

It was noted in a publication first published in 1968 and entitled *Life & Tradition in the Yorkshire Dales* that 'as far as can be judged, Irishmen have come to the Dales for hay-time for well over a hundred years, and were hired at local markets or at June Fairs such as those at Bentham or Skipton'.[50] It also appears that there is a long established traditional path between Mayo and the English midland farms of Yorkshire, Lancashire and Lincolnshire (traditionally seasonal migrants from Achill in Co. Mayo and Co. Donegal made Scotland their primary destination). In researching her book *Spalpeens and Tattie Hokers*, Anne O'Dowd interviewed several elderly former migratory labourers from two areas of Co. Mayo: the

Tattie hokers from Co. Mayo, Lincolnshire, 1950's. Courtesy of Des Ferguson.

first an area in west Mayo around Achill, Curraun and Belmullet, the second an area in east Mayo around Kiltimagh, Kilkelly, Straide and Swinford. The taped interviews were recorded in the early 1980s with men who had migrated to work for English farmers and a significant number of those interviewed had worked in Yorkshire. Thus it appears that Yorkshire was a traditional destination for Mayo's seasonal agricultural migrants. And information gleaned from the oral history accounts here would seem to confirm the existence of such a link. Of the respondents several had fathers, brothers and husbands who had initially come to Yorkshire as seasonal migrants in the early decades of the twentieth century. Both Bridget's father and eldest brother worked for farmers in the vicinity of Leeds, additionally her future husband along with many young men from his homeplace in north-east Mayo also worked in gangs as farm labourers around Yorkshire. Martin's father spent many seasons working on a big estate farm in a place called the Haws, Gunnerside in North Yorkshire:

It appears that Yorkshire was a traditional destination for Mayo's seasonal agricultural migrants

The thing of them days was like a crowd of lads from the village would go, 'bout might be ten or twelve like, would go from the village and go to England for the hay and the harvest like ya know and eh ... sometimes the spuds and the mangels [a large beet used to feed cattle] like ya know. And so there used to be the same crowd used to go, you know, year after year like ya know to England; and his last year was in 1947 like and I always remember then him then coming back you know like and he brought a horses collar home with him and he got a Raleigh bicycle for the girl like and I'll always remember him getting that and he got me something. But it was awful hard like was, you had to go to Skipton here in, in outside Leeds, it's about twenty miles outside Leeds a place called Skipton and that used to be for the hiring and all the farmers from all around North Yorkshire all the big farmers used to come there and all the Irish lads used to have to line up there and the farmer, the big farmers used to walk up and down the line and say 'I'll have you and I'll have you' and it was just like, ya know you've seen that thing called *Roots...* but they used always tried to get together those lads that was from the village like ya know used to like want to get to the one farmer, if not you know somewhere near each other. But then they used to be there brought out [sic] and then my father used to tell me how he used to sleep in the barn with the cattle, like you know, bed down with the hay like you know and sleep. This farmer, he used to tell me, had four sons and the first one would go out in the morning at six o'clock with them ya know and work like the clappers like ya know and he'd go back and he'd have his breakfast like you know then another fresh one would come down and that's how it was done all day you know those there who had rested would ... come out again in the afternoon and in the early evening you know to work the lads really to the core and you know it was all scythe work in them days as well you know like mowing with the scythe and everything and it was awful hard as he often described to me like ya know. But then probably on a Sunday they say they used to have to walk five or six miles to this church like you know that they used to like to go to and then they you know used to have a little drink but it was no bicycles or nothing it was all walking ya know, it was hard like ya know. But this farmer I always remember later on he used to send him a Christmas card every year you know like to keep in touch like you know even though my father wasn't going then you know when my father was older. But that's what they used to do like you know and they used to form a relationship sometimes like that you know and sometimes they were treated well like you know and more times there was, I suppose there was good and bad in everything like ya know but that was it like, you wouldn't get the young lads today to do that like. Thank goodness time has moved on. [Martin, b. 1940, Co. Mayo]

After a few seasons farm-labouring, particularly during the 1940s, many seasonal migrants gravitated to urban centres where all-year-round work could be found. Gradually more and more Irishmen were opting to work as part of Britain's army of workmen for its war effort; the pay was better, the working day and week were shorter, they could live in digs instead of in farm outhouses and be nearer to fellow Irishmen and the two central Irish institutions: the church and the public house. Another reason which affected the seasonal agricultural migrant's decision to turn to the cities for permanent work was that they were often denigrated by 'the townie'; John Healy observed 'the migratory farm worker was not an emigrant with any glamour or appeal'.[51] Often even the very words 'spalpeens' and 'tattie hokers' were used as terms of derision.[52] For those working on Yorkshire farms, Leeds was the main urban centre and thus the natural choice for work. The city was also situated at a midpoint for those who worked in agriculture in North Yorkshire, Lincolnshire in the east and Lancashire in the west.

It is a social truism that emigration begets emigration. Many respondents remarked that it appeared that everybody who was young and able was going to England, and influencing others by their actions:

Well, at that time everybody was goin' t'England; there was nothing else.
[Austin, b. 1916, Co. Roscommon]

Well everyone was comin' that time, all me mates was going away like... [Owen, b. 1943, Co. Mayo]

The *Reports of the Commission on Emigration* further remarked that the places in which Irish emigrants settled would lure prospective emigrants:

Recent emigration to Great Britain is building up centres of attraction in that country and, because of the facility of movement between the two countries, there is a danger that these may become magnets as powerful as the Irish centres in the United States in the 19th and early 20th centuries.[53]

Table 2.6: Irish-born Population in England: Selected Cities: 1951–81

City	1951	1961	1971	1981
London (a)	171,618 (b)	253,576 (b)	241,220	199,460
Birmingham	28,098	47,582	44,865	37,375
Manchester	16,280	24,577	23,040	18,135
Liverpool	14,122	12,006	8,470	5,759
Coventry	7,689	13,396	15,830	12,606
Leeds	4,788	6,632	7,580	7,563
Leicester	3,102	4,814	4,920	3,886
Sheffield	2,622	3,186	2,945	2,458
Nottingham	2,476	4,161	3,990	3,331
Luton	1,485	6,661	7,670	6,591
Northampton	1,336	2,357	2,915	2,458
Newcastle	1,326	1,356	1,040	1,093

Source: *Census of Population of England and Wales*: 1951–81, County Reports

Note: (a) Greater London; (b) Estimated

Census evidence supports this conjecture; the Irish population of cities such as London, Manchester, Birmingham, Coventry and Leeds for example increased dramatically between 1951 and 1971 (see Table 2.6). Liverpool is one notable exception. Furthermore, emigration to these cities facilitated further and continued emigration from Ireland, and authors of the *Reports* recognised that:

Tradition and example have also been very powerful influences ... For very many emigrants there was a traditional path 'from the known to the known', that is to say, from areas where they lived to places where their friends and relations awaited them.[54]

It became clear from the oral history interviews that although emigrants from every county in Ireland could be found in any British urban centre, certain towns and cities became associated with particular Irish counties. For example, Leeds is strongly associated with emigrants from Mayo and Donegal (but particularly the former), Huddersfield with emigrants from the Gaeltacht regions of Connemara and Kerry, and Sheffield with Galway.

There was a rake of men coming from Huddersfield [into Leeds] **that time, Connemara men that was their home that time, Connemara men like come to Huddersfield, it 'twas like the same in Leeds like Mayo men coming to Leeds, they had different towns o' coming to, ya see.** [Seamus, b. 1936, Co. Mayo]

Sheffield is a big Galway town. [Jeremiah, b. 1932, Co. Monaghan]

Thus emigrants from Mayo would follow their fellow countymen (and women) to Leeds because of its reputation as a 'Mayo town'. Before 1921, the census of England and Wales recorded the county of birth of Irish emigrants, thus we know that in 1861 18.1 per cent of the Irish in Leeds were born in Dublin, 8.9 per cent in Tipperary, 8.7 per cent in Queen's County and 7.3 per cent in Mayo, etc.[55] Since then, however, Irish-born persons living in Britain are sub-divided on the basis of whether they were born in the twenty-six or six counties. Therefore, it is only through oral testimony and personal memory that one can get a clear impression of the Irish composition of Leeds. By general consensus Leeds is long-recognised, from the 1930s at least, as being a Mayo town. Eithne recalls the Irish make-up of Leeds when she arrived in the early 1930s:

Oh they were from all parts; Mayo most of them in Leeds. [Eithne, b. 1911, Co. Mayo]

One Mayo veteran described his memories of being Irish in 1930s Leeds:

We were all very sensitive and unsure then. We'd cling together a lot with lads from our own county. After Mass we'd go to a pub in Leeds frequented by Mayo men. The talk would be mostly about Mayo and who was doing what back there – or about Mayo men here.[56]

Honora recalls of Leeds in the late 1930s that:

There was hardly any Galway people, except the Joyce's, they came over as tailors with my husband, they were here ... I think I knew only about four from Galway altogether, unless they were in other parts of the districts of Leeds. Everyone was from Mayo, every single one was from Mayo and they used all go to St Francis [Church Dancehall]**, that was out in Holbeck, was it, where was St Francis? Hunslet!** [Honora, b. 1914, Co. Galway]

Austin who moved to Leeds in 1938 recalls that:

There was a lot of Irish, like that they were from Connemara mostly, a lot of Mayo men in Leeds, you know, a lot of Mayos as well. But I didn't really know any of them at that time you know I was a kind o' a stranger even among me own like I didn't meet anyone that I knew from home there was nobody from Roscommon or from my place in Leeds at that time, in the later years they did come. [Austin, b. 1916, Co. Roscommon]

Additionally, Nuala and Gráinne attest to the fact that Leeds continued to attract Mayo men and women:

You know, I don't meet a lot of Wexford people you know, very few I've bumped into very few Wexford people, I think mostly all Mayo. [Nuala, b. 1931, Co. Wexford]

Donegal and Mayo took over Leeds, you know in the 70s an' 80s. Even in the Irish Centre they have the Donegal bar and they have the Mayo bar. [Gráinne, b. 1945, Co. Mayo]

This last remark refers to the Tara Suite, the main function room of the Leeds Irish Centre, in which there are two bars unofficially yet commonly known as the Mayo bar and the Donegal bar. Although by no means completely exclusive to either county they tend to attract their own countyfolk. This association of English cities with Irish counties is also supported by the writings of Donall Mac Amhlaigh who worked as a navvy in England in the mid-1950s:

I was working with another gang today for an hour or two ... three of the people I was with were from Galway City and they lived in Coventry. By all accounts, you'd be hard put to find any difference between the two cities, so many Galway people are in Coventry.[57]

In fact, the whole of West Yorkshire is recognised as having special connections with the western seaboard of Ireland and in particular 'is distinguished by the large numbers from County Mayo'.[58] In 1990, the Metropolitan District of Calderdale in West Yorkshire was officially twinned with Mayo. The Mayo-born Mayor of Calderdale, Councillor Joe Kneafsey, led a delegation from Yorkshire to Castlebar to sign a charter which it was hoped would lead to a stimulus in tourism and industrial activity in the two regions. The manager of the LIC, Mr Tommy McLoughlin, spoke of the benefits to emigrants from the west of Ireland who were arriving in Leeds:

Émigrés from Mayo and the western seaboard usually have family or friends in Leeds and other parts of Yorkshire who can help them to find their feet over the difficult first few months. It is the people from the east, from places like Dublin, who usually need the most help because they are less likely to have anyone established in the city to fall back on.[59]

One prominent member of the Leeds Irish Community went as far as to further sub-divide the Mayo composition of Leeds, stating that in fact the bulk of Irish emigrants in the city were from north Mayo:

I mean the most of the people in Leeds were from Swinford, Foxford, Crossmolina, Lahardaun, Belmullet, but then the absolute bulk of the Irish were from Attymass, Bonniconlon, Ballina, all this area, Killala, and then there was a minority then from, you might as well put south Mayo in with Kerry, Cork an' all the rest of the country, there was a spattering of people over from

**Map of County Mayo
showing principal
towns and villages**

Key to population

- Up to 500
- 500-3,000
- 3,000-10,000

Belderrig

Belmullet

Glenamoy

Ballycastle

Killala

Bangor

Crossmolina

Bonniconlon

Ballina

Attymass

SLIGO

Lahardaun

MAYO

Achill
Island

Foxford

Straide

Charlestown

Mulranney

Swinford

Newport

Castlebar

Kilkelly

Clew
Bay

Kiltimagh

Aghamore

ROSCOMMON

Westport

Knock

Ballyhaunis

Ballintubber

Claremorris

Tourmakeady

Ballinrobe

GALWAY

Cong

Roscommon but the bulk of the people were from here, from Attymass and Bonniconlon. [Michael, b. 1947, Leeds]

Undoubtedly the fact that emigrants from particular counties often had a preference for certain destinations had an effect on those Irish communities, occasionally resulting in inter-county rivalry and tension between fellow Irish emigrants. Oral evidence and personal testimony have shown that there was a predominance of emigrants from Co. Mayo in Leeds. It has been recognised that Irish emigrants retain a strong attachment to their native county.[60] Indeed it would appear that amongst the Irish loyalty to one's countymen often superseded loyalty to one's countrymen. Dillon noted that in mid-nineteenth century Leeds there was tension between Irish emigrants from particular counties.[61] A century later Donall Mac Amhlaigh in an autobiographical account of his time spent in Coventry in the 1950s detailed the conflict between the 'Connemara men and the people from Dublin. They've been fighting this many a day'.[62] This attachment accounts for the rise of the county association which have been described as the 'most important emigrant organisations' in twentieth century Britain and America.[63] Keeping with Mayo as the primary example, Mayo Associations were formed in New York and Philadelphia in the 1880s; today there are more than 20 Mayo Associations worldwide, in cities such as, for example, New York, Philadelphia, Boston, Chicago, San Francisco, Toronto, Sydney, London, Manchester, Coventry and not forgetting Leeds. The fact that Leeds had a strong Mayo contingency was beneficial for fellow Mayo emigrants in terms of securing employment and socialising; undoubtedly this encouraged further emigration from Mayo to Leeds and strengthened ties between the two communities. The flip side of course is that this domination could also pose problems for Irish emigrants who weren't from Mayo. Gráinne, from Mayo, recalled that:

There is a lot of people didn't like the Dubliners, they did not like Dublin. When I came over here first you'd hear people in the Shamrock at the dances saying the Dublin Jackeens they'd be calling them an' no they didn't like them ... and if anyone ever dared to go into the Mayo's and Donegal's area, that was it, they were "this is our area, you get out of it". [Gráinne, b. 1945, Co. Mayo]

And Thomas, being from Dublin, recalled feeling marginalised by his fellow countrymen in Leeds:

I mean the Irish community in Leeds was predominantly from Mayo, right? More than any other county so you know I must have known the name of every town in Mayo. And I did notice there was a kind of discrimination against you if you weren't from Mayo, yeah? That *did* exist.

BMcG: And what way do you think that manifested itself?

Oh, I don't mean in a nasty way particularly but you were kind of excluded, you know, to a certain degree. The Mayo people tended to be, or they were perceived to be kind of clannish, yeah? They were more interested in, you know, their own kind. And maybe I felt it because I was a Dubliner, as well you know. I remember there used to be an old Irish club in Leeds called the Irish National Club, and it closed down in about 1969 and they built the new Irish Centre and that opened in 1970 and this may have been partly imagination but I kinda got the impression that if you weren't from Mayo or the west of Ireland anyway you weren't quite as welcome in the Irish Centre. Nothing

was ever said directly like that, but you did get a few kind of sneers or you know kind of implied that you weren't so welcome. Partly it could have been imagination but I don't think it was fully that, you know, you *did* get that kind of an impression. There wasn't that many Dublin people in this town, there still isn't, you know, it's not a place where masses of Dublin people came to, you know, so there was kind of that, you were a Jackeen you know what I mean and that was it. It wasn't all that serious but there was a hint of that shall we say. [Thomas, b. 1941, Dublin]

It is perhaps unsurprising to learn that such a strong identification with ones native county often resulted in inter-county conflict and rivalry. This could be manifested in a number of ways. Liam recalls that there was much inter-county discrimination in Leeds particularly in the workplace; he clearly remembers a situation in which a group of Mayo men would not employ a close acquaintance of theirs simply because he did not hail from Mayo:

They wouldn't give him the start, they had the work but they wouldn't give him a job, oh they were very cliquish was the Mayo ... they had the upper hand all the way the Mayo lads, they definitely had. [Liam, b. 1934, Co. Wexford]

It was not uncommon to hear from male respondents that they secured employment in Leeds via a townie or a fellow countyman and also it was a common complaint that countymen tended to hire fellow countymen, particularly in the building trade.

Attachment to a particular county was intensified by one's absence from that county. One respondent Austin attributed the strong sense of homeplace amongst those emigrants from Mayo to their 'anthem' – the song the 'Boys from the County Mayo' – which was to be regularly heard in the public houses of Leeds. It has long been recognised that music can contribute to county identity:

In traditional music, various tunes have county names ... It is in popular and country music, however, that the county looms largest. There are such songs as 'Beautiful Meath', 'Moonlight in Mayo' and 'The Homes of Donegal' ... The association with place in song is most emotional when the emigrant is looking back to his or her native county. This is the Irish person's strong attachment to and rootedness in place, and the longing to be back home.[64]

Moreover in sport and romance tensions could run high between fellow emigrants. Martin recalls that Huddersfield tended to attract emigrants from the Gaeltacht regions of counties Kerry and Galway and that Gaelic football matches were occasionally played between emigrants from Huddersfield and Leeds:

So I used to play football up at Halton Moor, you see, Gaelic football on a Sunday and we used to play Huddersfield and there used to be hard games between Huddersfield and Leeds 'cause there was an awful lot of needle like ya know. And none of the Huddersfield lads liked you taking a girl, a Leeds lad taking a girl from Huddersfield. Oh Jesus ... oh they'd, they'd kill ya! [Martin, b. 1940, Co. Mayo]

In addition to being associated with Irish counties, certain British towns and cities became synonymous with certain types of work within Irish circles, particularly amongst Irish males. Since they were for the most part transient economic migrants in search of work it would seem logical that certain places would become associated with certain employment opportunities and this information would be disseminated within the Irish community in Britain. Edward emigrated from Dublin to Leicester in 1954, because he had heard talk of it:

But the trouble is that it were a woman's town, ya know nylon stockings an' shoes an' you know they wouldn't have had a lot of building, you know it hadn't been badly bombed. [Edward, b. 1933, Dublin]

Additionally, cities that had been heavily bombed during the war – Birmingham, Coventry, Liverpool, London and Sheffield – were all in desperate need of labourers for their reconstruction and thus they became associated with building work. In Yorkshire, traditionally Sheffield was synonymous with steelworks and Leeds with textiles. In the early decades of the twentieth century Leeds was primarily a textile and engineering city and was by all accounts heavily industrialised with plenty of employment opportunities in its countless mills, foundries and factories; in particular the city was strongly associated with the factory-made clothing industry. As with other British cities, the unskilled emigrant could secure employment in shops and restaurants, on trams and buses, in factories and mills, in domestic service or on construction sites. The economy of Leeds suffered a decline in the 1920s and 1930s, in particular in the heavy industries, and unemployment in the city was high.[65] However, in the inter-war years unemployment remained significantly below that of other major north of England centres – 17 per cent in 1930, peaking at 21 per cent in 1931 and falling to 9 per cent in 1937. Austin recalls that most Irishmen in Leeds in the 1930s were doing 'navvy-work':

You know it was all building then, there was building goin' on at the time. Now it was very bad up to the end of 1938 when the war clouds, then things began to brisk up because they knew there was war coming; now prior to that when I went there first you'd see notices up in factories 'No Irish Need Apply' and then all of a sudden that changed from 'Irishmen Wanted'. You know it amazing, you know, how they could change so quick when it suits them like … you weren't wanted, you were given to understand there, it was there for you to read 'No Irishman Need Apply' and then all of a sudden 'Irishmen Wanted'. Anyone unless you were stupid would know why you were wanted, because there were war coming; they wanted ya, not just in there at the factory, they wanted ya, what was meant by that was that they wanted ya in the army. [Austin, b. 1916, Co. Roscommon]

High male unemployment, economic depression and social tensions caused resentment towards the Irish in the workforce, and thus the identification of 'Irish' with 'outsider' was intensified. Austin, however, saw no specific malice towards the Irish in these kinds of notices; he believes that at times when jobs were scarce in Leeds in the 1930s it was only natural for the English to want to hire their own people:

Of course unemployment was rife at the time and the English people they wanted jobs and the idea of taking on these Irishmen, these rebels from Ireland, and all these so and so's that caused us all the trouble, you see they looked at it that we caused them a lot of trouble … the English people were nice but if it come to that an Englishman wanted a job down in the factory, it was a different story like, you couldn't blame 'em in a way like if he wanted the job. Well that's it, he'd have to be there in preference to an Irishman, wouldn't he? [Austin, b. 1916, Co. Roscommon]

Leeds, however, was notably prosperous in the 1950s, 1960s and early 1970s with a remarkably low unemployment level at less than 1 per cent in the boom years of 1955, 1961 and 1965 (levels that can be greatly contrasted to the 21 per cent of 1931). [66] This is despite the fact that the city's manufacturing base was in gradual decline from the 1920s to the 1970s; this decline was offset by the rise of an array of service industries:

While employment in mainstream engineering remained static, sharp declines in employment in metal and vehicle manufacture, textiles, clothing and footwear were more than counter balanced by rapid growth in building, gas, electricity and water, the distributive trades, insurance and banking, professional and scientific services and miscellaneous services. Between 1951 and 1973 while 37,000 jobs were lost in manufacturing, 32,000 jobs were gained in the service industries.[67]

Thus for the majority of the period under study many Irish men and women were attracted to Leeds by the availability and variety of work:

Leeds was good for work, part of the time, there now after the war. They were trying to build up and they had to do something, the wages weren't great but ... there were all types of work then, Irish lads mostly and it was all in the building trade.
[Austin, b. 1916, Co. Roscommon]

Well that time, that was the late fifties, early sixties, you could get...have a different job every day of the week that time ... Oh I'd jump around from Wimpeys, McAlpines, worked for UK, United Kingdom, that was underground gas-mains, putting underground gas-mains in. Then I went with Green Murphy's, jumping around with different firms.
[Vincent, b. 1939, Co. Galway]

We was in cloud nine, ya know, at that time, ya know, in the sixties the Irish was prospering and everything and really building and there was great lots of work going on construction, there was motorways being built and everything was booming in the sixties here like, ya know, and you couldn't be out of work I mean you'd have to been as lazy as sin not to have a job.
[Martin, b. 1940, Co. Mayo]

You just walked into the pub and got the start in the morning, no problem at all. [Timothy, b. 1944, Co. Kerry]

However, by the mid-1970s the unemployment figures began to reflect the continued decline in the manufacturing industry; in January 1976 unemployment in the city had risen to 5.5 per cent.[68] Yet when compared to national standards Leeds fared favourably in the 1980s and 1990s.

Another reason for moving to Leeds was to follow family and friends who were settled there. Family, relations and friends in Britain were important not only as an example to others who wished to emigrate but also as they provided support and encouragement. Several of the respondents had friends or relatives already living in Leeds when they arrived in the city and in many cases this was the primary reason why the city was their chosen destination.

The reason we came to Leeds, it could have been anywhere but it was Leeds because my father had a younger brother who lived here ... otherwise it could have been anywhere, Liverpool, London, Manchester or wherever; and I've lived in Leeds ever since, we came here in 1955. [Thomas, b. 1941, Dublin]

I came in the first place because it was just a family friend that was here, because I didn't know where to go and I just thought Leeds. I heard everybody talking about Leeds. [Gráinne, b. 1945, Co. Mayo]

Family emigration networks were of great importance amongst the respondents. For Eileen, Leeds was the obvious choice of destination; she had three siblings in England, two of whom were living in Leeds:

And she [mother] **said 'What do you want to do now?' I said 'I want to go to England, I want to go over to our Annie', me sister, 'cause I had Jackie an' Annie here at the time, me brother, an' I had Jim here, you know they never waited at home, they all, well there wasn't room for them, the lot of them. So I went to England when I was seventeen,** [19]**35.** [Eileen, b. 1918, Co. Mayo]

Eileen moved in with her sister in digs on arrival. Austin followed his future wife to Leeds; he had been working in Chester when she emigrated from Roscommon to cousins in the city:

Me wife now, God rest her, she was in Leeds then and I went to Leeds and I stayed with friends of hers as well. [Austin, b. 1916, Co. Roscommon]

Agnes arrived in Liverpool on a whim in 1938 but soon made her way to Leeds:

And this cousin of mine, she got to know I was here ... and she got in touch with me [so] **I came to Leeds.** [Agnes, b. 1918, Co. Roscommon]

Austin's daughter, Theresa, recalls the sequence of events that led to the eventual emigration of the whole family and the support network in Leeds that influenced their decision to leave Ireland:

I tell a lie, there was once I went on holidays to Leeds with mam in 1959 and I was there for about five weeks. I stayed with an aunt of mine, well there was plenty of 'em in Leeds so ... and while we were in England Johnny [brother] decided to move to England, he thought it was his best opportunity because he knew that if he left while mam was still in the house there'd be, you know, she'd be so emotional, because it was desperate when Timmy left ... as it turned out we went to England three years later ... My two older brothers were in Leeds, the next brother then was twenty, so I suppose they would have automatically come, that he would go as well an' I think in general there was encouragement from England as well to come over, the wonderful life in England, ya know. I would have known later that that encouragement had been there not beforehand but later I would have known that that encouragement was coming. Dad went over on a couple of holidays himself and he he'd got great encouragement while he was there – come over to England, bring the family over they'll have better opportunities, this, that and the other – and so he was kind of drawn to that then and also like what he said himself since is that he could see in the future that we would have all been gone and there'd be just himself and mam there and the way mam felt about the family being away would it not be better if we were all together an' move over, it seemed a logical kind of an answer to the whole thing. I think that's why mam went along with it 'cause she would have her family together but as it turned out Paddy [brother] didn't come with us, he didn't go with us, he lived at home for two more years and then he got to a point where he didn't have a choice, he had to go to England and that was that. So it was that way, that's basically how that happened.

BMcG: And did you have family or friends waiting there for you when you got over?

Yeah, well Timmy and Johnny were in the house, the house that we went to, Timmy and Johnny were actually living in that house. I had an aunt in Leeds who bought houses and rented them out to people and things like that, she was big into that type of thing, so she had found this house and they had gone in living to it before we went over so that's where we went. It was around the Chapeltown area. The accommodation was there, and initially when we went there dad went on the building sites out I suppose with my brother Johnny at the time but then he joined the post office shortly after. [Theresa, b. 1950, Co. Roscommon]

The emigrant's transition could be made easier by accessing an established network in the city. Friends and relations facilitated the move across the Irish Sea and provided practical support, helping out with accommodation and securing employment. Owen's recollections highlight the advantages to the greenhorn of having contacts in the city:

I came to the other side of the town now to here, Hyde Park, an' into a digs in Brudenell Mount that's in beside Hyde Park Corner; that was sixty, 1960, yeah Hyde Park Corner. The first morning I remember coming over an' I was standing at the bus-stop along with me brother, the brother was here a year before me or so an' I was looking up at the bus-stop like that an' I seen LST [sic] written up on the bus-stop an' I says 'What's LST [sic] mean?' 'Leeds fuckin' City Transport' Hughie said 'Don't let anybody hear ya saying that' [laughs]. Liam McDonnell was labour manager over Yorkshire an' he was a townie of mine then an' he got me into work straight away. [Owen, b. 1943, Co. Mayo]

Many respondents told how once they had settled family members and relatives followed in their footsteps and came to Leeds; they in turn were able to provide or help with finding accommodation. Following the death of Eileen's mother her younger siblings came from Galway to live with her and her husband in Leeds. And Bridget told how her and her husband's siblings, nieces and nephews arrived in Leeds, initially or permanently staying in their home; they often worked as labourers with her husband's small construction firm. Therefore, having family and kin in Leeds often determined this city as an initial destination since accommodation was immediately available.

Irish pubs, often known as 'Paddy's Exchange', were also important as places where accommodation and employment could be found

However, it wasn't necessary to have family and friends in Leeds to succeed in finding work and employment; Irish pubs, often known as 'Paddy's Exchange', were also important as places where accommodation and employment could be found. Seamus first arrived in Leeds from Euston Station, London, in 1964:

I got into Leeds on a Saturday, Saturday morning early and I fell asleep below at the railway station, I didn't know Leeds but I knew I heard them on about Chapeltown an' I asked this man where is Chapeltown, I didn't know Leeds. Oh he said 'you go up there an' you'll get a bus, do you know Chapeltown?' 'I don't' I said 'I never been in Leeds'. An' I made me way up about half-eleven an' I went into this pub, it was an Irish pub, there's a song about it – if ya want to go to go to work or meet the Irish that was the what do you call it, come to Chapeltown to the Roscoe – an' I went in there an' I met a few fellas in there. This Leeds was fill with work then, Leeds, in Leeds. I went in an' I met these two fellas an' I started talking to them, one of them was from Ballina, Murray was his name, an' this other fella was Grannon, he was from around Ballina an' all too. An' they were off on Saturday; drink was cheap then, I said 'Are ya having a drink?' 'cause they hadn't a lot of money, they were working out with Layden and a few others, I bought a drink an' they said to me 'We haven't seen you before' I said 'no, I just came into Leeds'. 'Well' they said 'you come into a good town, there's plenty o' work in it'. He said 'We're working, I'm a ganger' he said 'I'm a gangerman'. Murray, a cap on him, they had a nickname on him, they called him the horsheen Murray, he was an awful busy little man ... he said 'Well, if you go up now, drink that pint, it won't take you long, in about twenty minutes' he said 'and you'll be down here again, go up to Francis Street 25' he says 'an' you'll get a room'. He said 'We're living there an' I'll put you to work on Monday'. [Seamus, b. 1936, Co. Mayo]

Seamus got a room for twenty-five shillings a week in the lodging house, which was run by an old Polish couple

Seamus got a room for twenty-five shillings a week in the lodging house, which was run by an old Polish couple, and ended up in The Shamrock that same night with his newfound friends.

Leaving Home

The respondents were asked how they felt when they initially left home for England. In response to this question Owen articulated:

Oh well, I felt lonesome like you know leaving, well I didn't feel lonesome the first year I'll tell ya the truth, I didn't, I was too excited, dya' know, but after spending a few years here then and going back and coming over again you be sort of lonesome because you knew what was there for ya like ya know, there was Murphy's graft and fork an' a big bastard o' a gangerman roaring and shouting there at ya all day long if you weren't pulling yer weight and ya knew you had to work like. [Owen, b. 1943, Co. Mayo]

Austin recalled an emigration poem which for him summed up his experience of leaving:

Ah, no I didn't [mind going to England the first time]**, it didn't worry me, no not in the least no. I did mind leaving home, I felt very sad for me mother you know and all that kind of thing because there was a poem about that wasn't it, what was it? 'My father blessed me fervently but little did yet complain, but solely will me mother sigh till I come back again'. I did feel a bit put out about me mother like, because I knew me father felt me going like saddened but he wouldn't show it.** [Austin, b. 1916, Co. Roscommon]

His concern was not about what lay before him but about his parents and the loneliness they felt at his departure. Owen's remark that 'I didn't feel lonesome the first year' and Austin's that 'I didn't mind, it didn't worry me' were common responses from those interviewed. Many were too excited at the prospect of meeting up with family and friends already departed and of the thoughts of the impending freedom, nightlife and high wages they had heard so much about from returned emigrants. Gráinne recalls that she initially:

Thought tha' everything was brilliant, that it was so new to me, that I could go dancing an' [laughs]**, Friday, Saturday and Sundays. The Shamrock and St Francis's and then oh I thought it was great.** [Gráinne, b. 1945, Co. Mayo]

However, several of the respondents qualified their remarks by adding that after a number of years of coming home on holidays they became less and less eager to return to England. Owen's words counter the opinion of the emigration commissioners that emigrants 'find an easy alternative in emigration'.[69] Indeed the renowned playwright John B. Keane, who had first-hand experience of emigration, acutely observed this transition in his emotive musical play *Many Young Men of Twenty* in which the character Danger Mulally remarks:

I'll watch hundreds o' 'em goin' back again till the summer's over – back to their night shifts, an' filthy digs an' thievin' landladies. I'll be lookin' at them with their long faces leanin' out o' the carriage windows, with all their hard-earned money gone, an' their hearts broke with the thoughts of what's waitin' over. 'Tisn't so bad this time. This time it's an adventure. But wait till ye'll be goin' back the next time an' the time after that an' the time after that again. 'Twon't be an adventure then.[70]

Keane was well aware of the loneliness of emigration, having spent two years in England in the 1950s; Keane's *Self-Portrait* deals in part with his days in Northampton and London:

All around us as we left Dun Laoghaire, there was drunkenness. The younger men were drunk – not violently so but tragically so, as I was, to forget the dreadful loneliness of having to leave home … For us, as it was then, it was the brink of hell and don't think I use the word lightly![71]

John O'Donohue, too, wrote of the loneliness of those leaving Ireland for England: 'hundreds of people, young and old, with red eyes and lonesome faces'; whilst Donall Mac Amhlaigh penned that his heart felt like 'a solid black mass inside [his] breast'.[72]

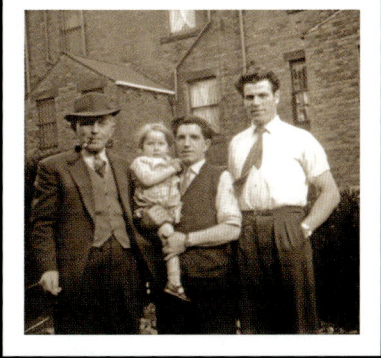

Landlord, Landlady and
Lodgers, Harehills, c. 1960.

Courtesy of Margaret
Jane Hegarty

Arriving in Leeds

As discussed in chapter three, Leeds established itself as a commercial centre of note in the nineteenth century. However, the cost of this industrial growth was that social and living conditions in the town deteriorated rapidly. The public face of Leeds was gradually and laboriously transformed from the 1870s; slums were cleared, sanitation was extended, the appearance and width of the town's streets were improved and public services and amenities were expanded. Leeds also possessed ultramodern transport and communications systems. The town had an efficient tramway system from the late 1800s; by 1936 the bus was fast becoming the dominant mode of public transport, with 170 kilometres of bus routes, eventually making the tram redundant in 1959.[73] In 1918, the largest automatic telephone exchange in Europe was opened in Leeds with 6,800 initial subscribers. In 1928 Leeds became the first English city to install automatic traffic lights. Leeds Corporation Gas Department was long since providing cheap gas for heating, lighting, cooking and for industry and by 1937 Leeds Corporation was supplying electricity to 148,194 customers.[74] Also the townspeople of Leeds were gradually replacing the old hobs and ranges with gas cookers. The city centre received a face lift in the early decades of the twentieth century; the present-day Headrow, Leeds' one kilometre long and twenty-seven metre wide main avenue, was refurbished in 1927 at an estimated cost of half a million pounds and in 1932 Lewis's state-of-the-art department store was opened on the Headrow at a cost of one million pounds.[75] The city centre also contained numerous Victorian shopping arcades, department stores, markets, cocoa houses, coffee shops, cafés and restaurants, cinemas, ballrooms, etc.

For those arriving from a comparatively 'backward' Ireland, Leeds was a different world; even in the 1930s Leeds was as advanced and as modern a city as could be found anywhere in the British Isles and seemed wondrous to newly arrived Irish emigrants, particularly for those who had come directly from rural Ireland. As wondrous as Leeds may have been to the new arrivals, the vast majority of the respondents have poor first impressions of the city. For all its wealth and urban splendour Leeds was a city literally blackened by its industrial base; smoke and smog in the city centre killed its trees and stained its statues and buildings. Smoke pollution in Leeds was a serious problem from the early nineteenth century; however, it wasn't until the 1970s that the use of smokeless fuels began to alleviate the situation. In 1921 the *Yorkshire Evening News* noted that 'Smoke and Leeds are almost as inseparably connected in the public mind as bacon and eggs'.[76] The dominant memory of the city for those who arrived in Leeds between the 1930s and 1960s is one of a dirty, smoky, malodorous and over-industrialised urban sprawl:

That was 1938 ... Leeds was, I'll tell ya what it was I hated it for one thing the smell of gas was horrible in it at that time. You know gas to a countryman then, that was brought up in the country, was horrible; people that were born and reared there wouldn't notice it you see but I hated the smell of gas it was horrible. [Austin, b. 1916, Co. Roscommon]

But was I sorry [laughs], I hated it, I detested it, them days [late 1930s] there was no such thing as a blue sky, it was black with soot and muck, even the footpaths were black with muck, the walls were black with muck, it was a terrible. It was, what do you call, an industrial city, and I couldn't understand why it was so black. And if ya went outside with a white coat on ya or a white dress you had to wash it the minute you come in, it was all smut, it was terrible. [Eileen, b. 1918, Co. Mayo]

It was as black with soot and muck, you couldn't see your hand ... you had to keep the doors closed, with the filth and the muck and the soot coming in. [Honora, b. 1914, Co. Galway]

It was always known as 'Mucky Leeds' in my time, my early time [1930s]. [Austin, b. 1916, Co. Roscommon]

When Honora followed her husband to Leeds in 1938, she arrived in Wellington Station and inquired about all the black buildings in the city in contrast to the whitewashed cottages that littered her native rural Galway:

Anyways I says to my husband 'Why do they paint everything black 'ere?' So Christy Joyce said 'Jaysus Christ Honora' he said 'that's filth, you'll know 'bout it when you're 'ere, that's filth.' And do you know you couldn't put your clothes out on a Monday morning because we were in between three hospitals an' in them days they hadn't these disposal things they used to burn everything in a big furnace and take the top of the chimney and let it all out ... oh the fog, we were lost, oh we were lost, once I went out ya know and I had a torch, a little torch an' during the war ya had a hood over it you couldn't show any light ya know an' I got lost an' I was going around an' they were all out looking for me. An' I was only in two streets away from our own house and I couldn't find me way home; it was scary, it was really scary, it was. [Honora, b. 1914, Co. Galway]

Even for those who came from Dublin, the Republic's most industrialised centre, the smog in Leeds was hard to take; Edward, who was brought up in the Liberties in central Dublin, arrived in Leeds in 1957 and recalls that:

When we come to Leeds it were awful you know smog and fog and you know we couldn't breathe sometimes, could we mam [wife]**? Everything were black you know.** [Edward, b. 1933, Dublin]

The situation worsened during the winter months when the city's thousands of coal fires were lit to stave off the bitter cold. Those living in the inner city faired worse as the smog settled in these lower lying areas. These areas were characterised by heavy industry and high concentrations of immigrants, including the Irish. Lawrence recalls:

When the fog hit there wasn't an air ... there wasn't a tree or a bush or a plant living down in Chapeltown. [Lawrence, b. 1950, Co. Donegal]

However, it wasn't merely the air pollution to which the emigrant had to adapt. Paschal, who arrived in the city in 1963 from west Mayo remembers the openness of his native rural homeplace and the claustrophobic feeling of urban Leeds:

When I come to Leeds the first day an' I got this digs down in Blackman Lane in Leeds an' looked out the window an' I seen all these bloody roofs, no grass and no trees from me and I couldn't see no relations, I tell you something I was as well off as if I was in jail, there'd be no difference. It was shocking; if I'd have had enough money I'd have gone home again. But I'd left no money to go back. [Paschal, b. 1944, Co. Mayo]

For natives of Dublin, or other Irish cities or larger county towns, the move to another urban area was perhaps less traumatic:

It was probably different for me because I was well used to cities anyway, you know, and essentially Leeds and Dublin weren't that different, you know, I was used to sort of buses, trams, houses, cinemas, all that kind of stuff. I think it would have been a lot different for somebody from say you know the depths of Mayo or Galway maybe miles away from the nearest town you know it was probably a different experience, so I didn't find it all that daunting in that sense. [Thomas, b. 1941, Dublin]

Urbanised Leeds often came as a shock to the emigrant's system, particularly to those who had never travelled outside their own rural environment. Martin and Eamonn arrived in Leeds as children in 1949 and 1961 respectively:

[We] had got a house just in a place called Copton Place, Leeds 2, its just in the middle of the ring road now, it was only a stones throw from St Anne's Cathedral and I always remember we went down to half nine Mass on the Sunday morning, it was a huge church like you know I had never seen such big buildings in all me life like you know because coming from the rural like you only just seen odd houses like but there was all these terraced houses joined together. [Martin, b. 1940, Co. Mayo]

We come over like [1961] and the shock, the culture shock of coming from a place like that [Mayo] coming into Leeds, well that hit me hard, it couldn't have hit me harder like you know ... coming out of Leeds city centre and you get these big massive cars, buses, I never seen 'ought like that in me life before, like you know, cars, buses and people running about and there thousands of people like. I've still got that memory to this day actually. [Eamonn, b. 1952, Co. Mayo]

Owen's recollections of rural Mayo in the 1950s contrast greatly with the above memories of modern urban Leeds in the 1930s; it would appear to anyone who had experienced both that Ireland was caught in a time-warp untouched by the advancements of the modern world:

When I was young if we seen a train we'd nearly jump in front of it, or a car on the road, you'd never see a car on the road hardly. I remember the first car I seen on the road, I do yeah. An' I remember the first black man I seen, in at the fair-day in Foxford, we were round about after him all day long, wondering what sort of a fuckin' man he was weighing him up an' looking at him and rubbing him to see would ya, was it paint or what was it. [Owen, b. 1943, Co. Mayo]

Whilst some of the respondents remember settling in to city life with relative ease, especially if they had family and friends in the city, others were initially very lonely:

I had no problem settling in because it was full board I went into, and me brother was in the house and three or four more lads that I knew but there was lads there now, there was this Mossy Gallagher and he didn't come out o' the room or come out for anything to eat for nearly a fortnight after him coming over ... because he was lonesome, that lonesome. [Owen, b. 1943, Co. Mayo]

I was over here one week and I hated it, every minute of it ... I just got home sick. [Margaret, b. 1955, Co. Mayo]

However, Eileen recalls that having family in Leeds didn't always ensure that the emigrant would feel at home in their new urban home:

I got homesick after six weeks and Annie [sister] had the doctor into me and all this, we lived in Compton Road at the time, two nice old ladies, two widows, and they were lovely and they treated me as a baby you see, but I was very ill and they called the doctor in, the doctor in, three weeks in bed and nothing wrong with me just being homesick an' me sister said 'you'll have to go to work, we cannot keep ya any longer', she had to pay me board, so and I think that was twelve shillings a week then, so I went to work ... she said 'there's no money for ya to go home, I have no money to send ya home so you'll have to stay.' So I had to stay didn't I? [Eileen, b. 1918, Co. Mayo]

Many respondents expressed having some communication difficulties when they initially arrived in Leeds because of the 'broad' Yorkshire accent:

I do remember my Dublin accent, you know, being teased about my accent and wondering why I was being teased when they weren't speaking English at all, the natives, as far as I was concerned; I had great difficulty in understanding the Yorkshire accent, you know. [Thomas, b. 1941, Dublin]

Since English was the first language of the majority of Irish emigrants, it is easy to dismiss the fact that there was a communication barrier, or rather a dialect barrier, between emigrant and native: between Hiberno-English and Yorkshire Dialect. As the following extract highlights, certain Hiberno-English idiosyncrasies were passed onto English-born children of Irish emigrants and that this could identify that a child was of Irish stock:

There was a difference in the speech of the children of the Irish people, intonations and turns of the tongue that their Yorkshire bred companions had not. Often a friend of Mary's would try to correct her speech ... 'Why do you say "She does be coming down the street?" Can't you say, "She's cuming down t' street?" That's the reight way to speak English!' Or, 'Why do you Irish always say "the"? "Close the door! Here's the box." Don't you know you should say Shut t' door – Here's t' box?' – It's only the Irish that say "the"![77]

Language is indicative of identity; in an autobiographical account, one Chilean expatriate wrote of his linguistic displacement that: 'I wanted someone to understand what it is like to see your life suddenly cut down, your points of reference blurred, your ability to express emotions and feelings impaired by the pervasive presence of a different culture and language'.[78] However, dialect and accent are also potent indicators of identity. The Yorkshire Dialect, which has its own idiosyncratic grammar and distinct pronunciation and is littered with Saxon, Old Norse and Icelandic words, often proved difficult for the uninitiated. Many of the respondents spoke of the difficulties in both understanding and being understood by Leeds natives. Yorkshire folk commonly used 'lass' and 'lad' for girl and boy, 'aye' and 'nay' for yes and no; one humourous observation on Yorkshire Dialect was made by William Benn in his work *Wortley-de-Leeds*: 'Two men met at the Exchange [Employment Centre], one said "Owt?" and the other said "Nowt", and they passed on',[79] 'owt' means anything and 'nowt' means nothing. Martin arrived in the city, aged nine, from rural Mayo:

It was a very, very, very hard to be honest like ya know ... you come from such a rural part of Ireland and to come to such an environment of everything, big monstrosities of buildings like you know and then there also was also the accent, the Yorkshire accent is improved a lot now that you don't hear as much, but for 'water' like, as we would say at the time, was 'watta' ya know and awful lingo it was like very hard to understand like ya know I found it awful, awful hard that like ya know to understand the accent like ya know it was terribly hard was that ... and all you heard in the morning when you went in was 'did thou see telly last neet?' you know 'did thou watch that programme ont' telly last neet?' and that's the way they used to talk. [Martin, b. 1940, Co. Mayo]

Eamonn was also very young when his family left Mayo for Leeds; he arrived in the city in 1961, aged nine; he recalls his Irish accent being ridiculed in school, so much so that he consciously mimicked the city accent:

And the biggest thing, culture shock I got were when I end up going to school and I had this accent a really, you know, strong ... well that was it, you stood out like a sore thumb like you know like and I really got, I didn't really like it you know you got called a Paddy. [Eamonn, b. 1952, Co. Mayo]

Linguistic scholars have noted 'that recent years have seen a marked decline in the use of the traditional dialects of Yorkshire'.[80] The decline can be attributed to a number of factors, some of which have also been instrumental in the decline in use of Hiberno-English.[81] These factors include the influence of Standard English and the media's tendency to use uniformity of vocabulary. Social changes and geographical mobility have also eroded regional diversity. Additionally, education, with its focus upon Standard English and its intolerance of non-standard varieties of the language, and the social attitude that associates Standard English with breeding and intelligence, have contributed to the decline of Yorkshire Dialect. Martin has witnessed this change over the last half-century:

But it's not as much noticeable now even ... you wouldn't notice it as much now as we did fifty years ago when we come here like so because they've improved themselves has the Yorkshire people like ya know speaking better but there was 'watta' [water] and 'nowt' [nothing] and all that sort of craic, ya know. And it was so difficult to understand from our way of talking. [Martin, b. 1940, Co. Mayo]

The vast majority of the respondents have retained a distinct Irish accent, although an occasional word sometimes betrays the fact that they have lived in Britain for most of their lives.

Additionally, the linguistic transition must have been compounded for emigrants from the Gaeltacht who had little or no English. Bríd Duggan, the Leeds 'Lady Mayoress of the Occasion' and a native of Co. Galway recalls the difficulties encountered by those who arrived in Leeds from Irish speaking areas without the English language: 'I felt very isolated. I couldn't read the newspapers, street signs, cooking instructions on cans of food – all the things we generally take for granted'.[82] Gráinne recalls that those from the Gaeltacht were also often ostracised from their fellow Irish:

The Connemaras, I know a lot of people couldn't get on with them, a lot of people couldn't get on with them. They were very fiery, very fiery, especially if they had a few drinks on them. And they seemed to be really, really clannish. And they were the Gaeltacht they spoke a lot of Irish there you see and I think that would be it. [Gráinne, b. 1945, Co. Mayo]

There were of course other social changes to adapt to also; one of the most common remarks was that most of the respondents had never seen a black person before arriving in Britain. As a result of active recruiting in the Caribbean colonies in order to fill lower-paid jobs, Leeds along with other large British cities witnessed an increase in foreign immigration in the late 1950s. By 1961 2.7 per cent of the population was born overseas, of whom around half were from Commonwealth countries.[83]

In the afternoon we went out for a walk to explore around the area like you know and I seen this black man, the first one I'd ever seen and I let this roar out I said 'Hey, look, look a black man' and I never knew that there was such a thing existed to be honest like I didn't and the next thing you know I got me ear pulled and I could see these big white eyes of this black fella like looking over across the road like you know and Jasus but I was soon chastised for saying that like but I never knew there was such a black man in me life, I never seen one like, it seems so funny today like but anyways. [Martin, b. 1940, Co. Mayo]

Eventually the emigrant was faced with three choices: to return home to Ireland, to adapt to urban life and make new lives in the city or to stay and tolerate their predicament.

At first I was a bit dubious, you know, I thought every week I was going to leave, I wasn't going to stop but then I soon settled in. [Nuala, b. 1931, Co. Wexford]

Without doubt some returned to Ireland after a short or long duration in the city, many more settled in and established themselves in the city after an initial adjustment period.

Notes

1 Alistair Thomson, 'Moving Stories: Oral History and Migration Studies', *Oral History: Migration*, vol. 27, no. 1, spring 1999, p. 28.

2 R. F. Foster, *Modern Ireland, 1600–1972*, 1989, p. 345.

3 C. J. Houston and W. J. Smyth, 'The Irish Diaspora: Emigration to the New World, 1720–1920', in B. J. Graham and L. J. Proudfoot (eds), *An Historical Geography of Ireland*, 1993, pp. 340-1.

4 Foster, Modern Ireland, 1600–1972, p. 348.

5 Houston and Smyth, 'The Irish Diaspora', p. 341.

6 King, Shuttleworth and Strachan, 'The Irish in Coventry', p. 65; Strachan, 'Post-war Migration and Settlement in England and Wales 1951–1981', pp. 21-2; and Enda Delaney, 'Almost a Class of Helots in an Alien Land', p. 241.

7 Séan Duffy (ed.), *The Atlas of Irish History*, 2000, p. 90.

8 P. J. Drudy, 'Migration Between Ireland and Britain Since Independence', in P. J. Drudy (ed.), *Irish Studies 5: Ireland and Britain Since 1922*, 1986, p. 107.

9 Drudy, 'Migration Between Ireland and Britain Since Independence', p. 107.

10 Terence Brown, *Ireland: A Social and Cultural History, 1922 to the Present*, 1995, p. 18.

11 Brown, *Ireland*, p. 18.

12 Tracey Connolly, 'Emigration from Ireland to Britain During the Second World War', in Andy Bielenberg (ed.), *The Irish Diaspora*, 2000, p. 51.

13 *Reports of the Commission on Emigration and Other Population Problems, 1948–54*, para. 8, 1956, p. 369.

14 Delaney, *Demography, State and Society*, p. 189.

15 *Irish Press*, 22 April 1948.

16 Pauric Travers, 'There Was Nothing for Me There: Irish Female Emigration, 1922-71', in Patrick O'Sullivan (ed.), *The Irish World Wide. Volume 4: Irish Women and Irish Migration*, p. 158–9.

17 *Reports of the Commission on Emigration and Other Population Problems, 1948–54*, para. 280, p. 130.

18 *Reports of the Commission on Emigration and Other Population Problems, 1948–54*, para. 280, p. 130.

19 *Reports of the Commission on Emigration and Other Population Problems, 1948–54*, para. 280, p. 130.

20 *Reports of the Commission on Emigration and Other Population Problems, 1948–54*, para. 282, p. 131.

21 Appendix 12 and 14 in Enda Delaney, *Demography, State and Society*, pp. 311-13.

22 John A. Jackson, *The Irish in Britain*, 1963, p. 81.

23 Travers, 'There Was Nothing for Me There', p. 149.

24 Bronwen Walter, 'Gender and Recent Irish Migration to Britain', *Geographical Society of Ireland Special Publications 6*, 1991, p. 11.

25 Lambert, *Irish Women in Lancashire, 1922-60*, pp. 12-13.

26 Peter Moser, 'Rural Economy and Female Emigration in the West of Ireland, 1936-56', *UCG Women's Studies Centre Review*, vol. 2, 1993, p. 47.

27 See Table 29 ('Age Distribution of Emigrants from the Whole of Ireland, 1852–1921') of the *Statistical Appendix of the Reports of the Commission on Emigration and Other Population Problems, 1948–54*, p. 320.

28 Delaney, *Demography, State and Society*, p. 48.

29 *Reports of the Commission on Emigration and Other Population Problems, 1948–54*, para. 276, p. 129.

30 Travers, 'There Was Nothing for Me There', p. 148.

31 Liam Ryan, 'Irish Emigration to Britain Since World War II', in Kearney, Richard (ed.), *Ireland: The Emigrant Nursery and the World Economy*, 1990, p. 46.

32 *Reports of the Commission on Emigration and Other Population Problems, 1948–54*, para. 290, p. 134.

33 *Reports of the Commission on Emigration and Other Population Problems, 1948–54*, para. 300, p. 137.

34 *Reports of the Commission on Emigration and Other Population Problems, 1948–54*, para. 300, p. 137.

35 Declan Kiberd, *Inventing Ireland: The Literature of the Modern Nation*, 1996, pp. 474-5.

36 Connolly, 'Emigration from Ireland to Britain During the Second World War', p. 58.

37 Quoted in Connolly, 'Emigration from Ireland to Britain During the Second World War', p. 58.

38 John Cannon (ed.), *The Oxford Companion to British History*, 1997, p. 973.

39 O'Connor, *The Irish in Britain*, p. 83.

40 Duffy (ed.), *The Atlas of Irish History*, p. 120.

41 Duffy (ed.), *The Atlas of Irish History*, p. 120.

42 *Reports of the Commission on Emigration and Other Population Problems, 1948–54*, para. 303, p. 138.

43 Moser, 'Rural Economy and Female Emigration in the West of Ireland, 1936-56', p. 41.

44 Joy Rudd, 'The Emigration of Irish Women', *Social Studies: Irish Journal of Sociology*, vol. 9, nos 3/4, spring 1987, p. 3.

45 *Investment in Education*, Dublin: Stationary Office, 1966.

46 John Healy, *No-one Shouted Stop! (Formerly Death of an Irish Town)*, 1988, p 15.

47 Jackson, *The Irish in Britain*, p. 28.

48 Sean Glynn, 'Irish Emigration to Britain, 1911-1951: Patterns and Policy', *Irish Economic and Social History*, VIII, 1981, p. 51.

49 Shants or Shanty's from the Irish seantán or sean tigh. These were usually farm out-houses converted, with little effort, to accommodate seasonal labourers.

50 Marie Hartley and Joan Ingilby, *Life & Tradition in the Yorkshire Dales*, 1973, p. 73.

51 Healy, *No-one Shouted Stop!*, p 15.

52 Anne O'Dowd, *Spalpeens and Tattie Hokers: History and Folklore of the Irish Migratory Agricultural Worker in Ireland and Britain*, 1990, p. 227.

53 *Reports of the Commission on Emigration and Other Population Problems, 1948–54*, para. 301, p. 137.

54 *Reports of the Commission on Emigration and Other Population Problems, 1948–54*, para. 301, p. 137.

55 Dillon, 'The Irish in Leeds, 1851–61', 1979.

56 Quoted in O'Connor, *The Irish in Britain*, pp. 72–3.

57 Donall Mac Amhlaigh, *An Irish Navvy: The Diary of an Exile*, 2003, p. 151.

58 Jim Moran, 'Goodbye and Good Riddance', *Yorkshire Post*, 2 April 1990.

59 Moran, 'Goodbye and Good Riddance'.

60 Mary E. Daly, 'The County in Irish History', in Mary E. Daly (ed.), *County and Town: One Hundred Years of Local Government in Ireland*, 1999, p. 1; and David A. Gillmor, 'The County: Designation, Identity and Loyalty', in Jim Hourihane (ed.), *Engaging Spaces: People, Place and Space from an Irish Perspective*, 2003, p. 46.

61 Dillon, 'The Irish in Leeds, 1851–61', p. 15.

62 Mac Amhlaigh, *An Irish Navvy*, p. 51.

63 Daly, 'The County in Irish History', p. 1.

64 Gillmor, 'The County', p. 55.

65 Burt and Grady, *The Illustrated History of Leeds*, p. 207.

66 Thornton, *Leeds: The Story of a City*, p. 231.

67 Burt and Grady, *The Illustrated History of Leeds*, p. 231.

68 Burt and Grady, *The Illustrated History of Leeds*, p. 231.

69 *Reports of the Commission on Emigration and Other Population Problems, 1948–54*, para. 295, p. 135

70 John B. Keane, *Many Young Men of Twenty, Moll, The Chastitute*, (no date), pp. 138–9.

71 Keane, *Self Portrait*, quoted in Bernard Canavan, 'Story-Tellers and Writers Irish identity in emigrant labourers' autobiographies, 1870–1970' in Patrick O'Sullivan (ed.), *The Irish Worldwide. Volume 3: The Creative Migrant*, 1994, p. 164.

72 Canavan, 'Story-tellers and Writers', p. 164.

73 Burt and Grady, *The Illustrated History of Leeds*, p. 212.

74 Burt and Grady, *The Illustrated History of Leeds*, p. 213.

75 Burt and Grady, *The Illustrated History of Leeds*, pp. 212–13.

76 *Yorkshire Evening News*, 26 Nov. 1921.

77 Patterson, *The Ham Shank*, p. 16.

78 Iván Jaksic, 'In Search of Safe Haven', in Rina Benmayor and Andor Skotnes (eds), *International Yearbook of Oral History and Life Stories, Vol. III, Migration and Identity*, 1994, p. 26, quoted in Alistair Thomson, 'Moving Stories: Oral History and Migration Studies', *Oral History: Migration,* vol. 27, no. 1, spring 1999, p. 34.

79 From William Benn, *Wortley-de-Leeds*, 1926. http://www.mv.y-net.com/lamb/yorks_dialect.htm. Accessed 1 March 2004.

80 P. French et al., 'Documenting Language Change in East Yorkshire', *Transactions of the Yorkshire Dialect Society*, vol. XVI, Part LXXXVI, 1986, p. 29.

81 These factors can be viewed in detail on the web-site entitled Yorkshire Dialect (http://www.yorksj.ac.uk/dialect/) which is maintained by Barry Rawling of the Department of Language Studies and Linguistic, School of Management, Community and Communication, The College of St John, York. The factors are, in the main, drawn from the following studies: P. Trudgill, *The Dialects of England*, 1990; J. Cheshire and J. Milroy, 'Syntactic Variation in Non-Standard Dialects: Background Issues', in Milroy and Milroy (eds), *Real English*; J. Cheshire and V. Edwards, 'Sociolinguistic in

the Classroom: Exploring Linguistic Diversity', in Milroy and Milroy (eds), *Real English*; A. Hughes and P. Trughill, *English Accents and Dialects*, 1996.

82 *Irish Examiner*, 18 Nov. 2000.

83 Burt and Grady, *The Illustrated History of Leeds*, p. 231.